C000097312

WALKS FOR ALL AGES
IN THE
SOUTH DOWNS
NATIONAL PARK

WALKS *FOR* *ALL* AGES

SOUTH DOWNS NATIONAL PARK

BRADWELL
BOOKS

Published by Bradwell Books
9 Orgreave Close Sheffield S13 9NP
Email: books@bradwellbooks.co.uk

Terry Owen asserts his rights to be identified as the author of walks 1, 2, 3, 4, 5, 6 and 7.
Keith McKenna and Sally Dench assert their rights to be identified as the authors of walks
8, 9, 10, 11, 12, 13, 14, 15 and 16.
Steve Davison asserts his rights to be identified as the author of walks 17, 18 and 19.
Hugh Taylor and Moira McCrossan assert their rights to be identified as the authors of
walk 20.
All rights reserved. No part of this publication may be reproduced, stored in a retrieval
system or transmitted in any form or by any means, electronic, mechanical, photocopying,
recording or otherwise without the prior permission of Bradwell Books.
British Library Cataloguing in Publication Data: a catalogue record for this book is available
from the British Library.

1st Edition

ISBN: 9781910551950

Design: Andy Caffrey
Edited by: Louise Maskill
Typesetting and mapping: Mark Titterton
Photograph credits: © Terry Owen; Keith McKenna and Sally Dench; Steve Davison; Hugh
Taylor and Moira McCrossan; iStock; South Downs National Park
Front cover image: iStock
Print: Gomer Press, Llandysul, Ceredigion SA44 4JL

Maps contain Ordnance Survey data
© Crown copyright and database right 2017
Ordnance Survey licence number 100039353

Bradwell Books and the authors have made all reasonable efforts to ensure that the details
are correct at the time of publication, and cannot accept responsibility for any changes
that have taken place subsequent to the book being published. It is the responsibility
of individuals undertaking any of the walks listed in this book to exercise due care and
consideration for their own health and wellbeing and that of others in their party. The walks
in this book are not especially strenuous, but individuals taking part should check the
appropriate weather forecast and ensure they are fit and well before setting off.

CONTENTS

THE SOUTH DOWNS NATIONAL PARK IS ENGLAND'S NEWEST NATIONAL PARK, COVERING OVER 600 SQUARE MILES OF CHALK DOWNLAND IN HAMPSHIRE AND SUSSEX AND THE WOODED HILLS AND VALES OF THE WESTERN WEALD. THE PARK WAS FULLY CREATED IN 2011 AFTER MANY YEARS OF CAMPAIGNING AND NEGOTIATION, TO PRESERVE THE SENSITIVE GEOLOGY AND ECOLOGY OF THE CHALK DOWNLAND, WOODS AND HEATHLAND. IT ENCOMPASSES TOWNS SUCH AS LEWES, PETERSFIELD AND MIDHURST ALONG WITH A WEALTH OF SMALLER VILLAGES AND HAMLETS, SOME OF WHICH YOU WILL VISIT DURING THE WALKS IN THIS BOOK.

The route along the tops of the chalk highlands was one of the few that were safely passable by Mesolithic Britons some 8000 years ago, above the densely forested valleys of the Weald and less hazardous and drier than the wetter lowlands. Since then the tracks and trails have been used (and fought over) by Neolithic, Iron Age, Roman and medieval peoples, all leaving evidence of their presence and their passing in the landscape and the archaeological record.

The area abounds with natural and social history, containing protected habitats rich in rare species as well as hillforts, Roman remains, battle sites and abandoned medieval villages – all alongside the thriving communities who make their homes here today. Many of the historic buildings and sites are owned or managed by national conservation organisations; the introductions and 'The Basics' sections for each of the walks will give you some pointers for what to look out for along the way, with abbreviations indicating ownership where applicable (NT: National Trust; EH: English Heritage; and HHA: Historic Houses Association).

The South Downs Way is one of Britain's 15 national trails, following a 100-mile route along the high chalk ridges of the national park. It was officially opened in 1972 as an 80-mile trail from Buriton in Hampshire to Beachy Head above Eastbourne in Sussex, and was extended some fifteen years later; it now starts in Winchester in Hampshire and concludes with a loop around Eastbourne, and is waymarked along its length by distinctive acorn signs indicating its national trail status. It involves just over 4000 metres of ascent and descent along its undulating 100 miles, and is popular with walkers, runners, cyclists and riders alike. For the most part the route follows bridle paths, with some sections on footpath and occasional short distances on roads or byways.

Many walkers plan through-trips from one end of the South Downs Way to the other, taking around 8 or 9 days to complete the 100-mile route with accommodation and camping opportunities plentiful along the way. However, walking short sections of the trail can be just as rewarding; many of the walks in this book include a section of the trail on their routes. The twenty walks, spaced along the trail and throughout the national park, have been carefully selected to give you a taste of all the different habitats and landscapes that the South Downs have to offer.

Enjoy walking the South Downs National Park with Bradwell Books!

FACT FILE

The information in this book has been produced in good faith and is intended as a general guide. Although the maps in this book are based on original Ordnance Survey (OS) mapping, walkers are always advised to use a detailed OS map. Look in 'The Basics' sections for recommendations for the most suitable OS Landranger and/or Explorer maps for each of the walks.

All the walks follow rights of way or paths open to the public, with occasional roadside paths (take care when crossing roads). The walks should be suitable for most people, especially families, ranging in length from around 2 to 6 miles. They are graded and described in 'The Basics' sections to help you select the most appropriate walks for your party.

A good pair of walking books is recommended, and it is advisable to take good-quality waterproofs and wear plenty of layers of warm clothing if indicated by the weather forecast. Suggestions for rest stops and refreshments are indicated in 'The Basics', but packing a snack and a drink is advisable. Dogs are welcome on all the walks, as long as they can manage stiles (as indicated in 'The Basics' sections) and are kept on leads near roads or when livestock may be present.

1 BEACHY HEAD

THIS IS A SPECTACULAR WALK ON THE ROLLING CLIFF TOPS ALONG BRITAIN'S HIGHEST CHALK SEA CLIFFS, WHICH CAN BE EXTENDED.

The name Beachy Head is derived from the corruption of the French beau chef or 'beautiful headland'. There can be no doubt it lives up to its name. The walk starts from the high point of the cliffs, recorded at 538 feet (164 metres), and the nearby Countryside Centre (free entry) provides a feel for the area before you set off. Nearby a Compass Rose shows the direction and distance to other parts of the UK and the world.

The Peace Path, created in 1987 to celebrate the United Nations International Year of Peace, is a short circular path around the headland and leads to a viewpoint. Close to the viewpoint stands a memorial erected in 2012 in memory of Bomber Command. Beachy Head lighthouse sits at the bottom of the cliffs. It was built in 1902 by Trinity House under the guidance of Sir Thomas Matthews, their engineer-in-chief. It replaced an earlier structure, Belle Tout lighthouse, 1½ miles further west. Built of 3,660 tons of Cornish granite the lighthouse stands 142 feet (43 metres) high and continues to serve the busy shipping lanes along the south coast. It was automated in 1983.

Belle Tout lighthouse was built in 1831 and became operational in 1834. The granite building replaced an even earlier structure that had been built by John 'Mad Jack' Fuller. As Squire of Brightling in East Sussex, he was called 'mad' because of the follies he built in and around the village of Brightling. A larger-than-life character, he served as High Sheriff of Sussex and had a turbulent career as a Member of Parliament: for Southampton from 1780 to 1784 and for Sussex from 1801 to 1812. Belle Tout passed through various private owners until 1999, when the then owners realised that cliff erosion was close to sending the building plunging into the sea. At great expense the building was raised and dragged 56 feet from the edge to temporary safety. Since then the building has undergone a total renovation, the gardens have been landscaped and a new approach drive laid down. It currently offers a unique location for bed and breakfast accommodation.

Most of the westward route of the walk follows the South Downs Way National Trail, which starts – or finishes, depending upon the direction chosen to walk this 100-mile trail – just a mile east on the edge of Eastbourne. The trail is marked with the National Trail 'acorn' marker on the waymark posts.

THE BASICS

Distance: 3 miles / 5km (5 miles / 8km if you follow the longer version of the walk)

Gradient: Undulating

Severity: Moderate

Approx. time to walk: 2½ hours (3½ hours for the longer route)

Stiles: Two

Maps: OS Explorer 123 (Eastbourne and Beachy Head); OS Landranger 199 (Eastbourne and Hastings)

Path description: Grass cliff top, field, chalk path

Start Point: Beachy Head car park (GR TV 591959)

Parking: Pay and display car parking adjacent to Beachy Head Countryside Centre (PC BN20 7YA)

Dog friendly: If they can manage stiles, and should be on leads

Public Toilets: At start in car park

Nearest food: Beachy Head Hotel adjacent to Beachy Head Countryside Centre. Pub and tea rooms at Birling Gap (2½ miles west of Beachy Head)

Look out for: Beachy Head Lighthouse (don't go too close to the edge), Belle Toute Lighthouse (now a bed-and-breakfast)

1 BEACHY HEAD WALK

ROUTE

1. From the Countryside Centre, carefully cross the road to the War Memorial. Bear right on a tarmac path (the Peace Path) to reach the viewpoint.

2. Leave the viewpoint and continue on the Peace Path until it begins to bear right to return to the start. At that point, turn left onto a clifftop path.

3. Continue along the cliff top; the path descends for about 0.75 miles (1 kilometre). If undertaking the longer route, continue as described in 11 to 13 (below).

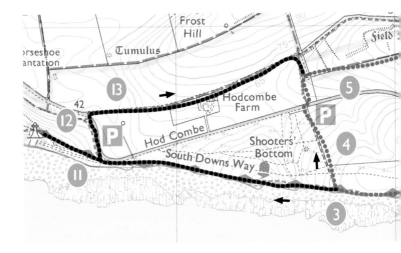

4. Otherwise, turn right and with scrub on the left gently descend to the road close to a car parking area on the left. Cross with care onto a bridleway opposite.

5. In about 100 metres at a path junction, turn right on a path over an area known as West Brow with a fence line on the left. Remain on the path, passing beneath the Countryside Centre on the right and Bullockdown Farm on the left.

6. Continue ahead over Heathy Brow, where the path levels out and bears left towards the corner of the field and a stile.

7. Emerge onto a farm track. Turn right, passing a dew pond on the right, and reach the road. Cross with care.

8. Bear half-right and descend towards a bench on the South Downs Way offering extensive views over Eastbourne and Pevensey Bay.

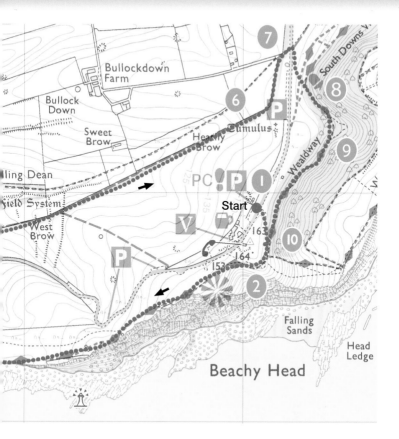

9. Turn right onto the South Downs Way and follow the marked path, which becomes narrow and passes through scrub.

10. Emerge onto an ascending path and onto the Peace Path again. Turn right to return to the start.

11. Longer route: from 3 (above), continue ahead (westwards) on the South Downs Way to meet with the road and car parking areas on the right. Continue ahead and ascend to reach Belle Tout lighthouse.

12. Retrace the route, but before reaching the road again turn left onto a path that follows the line of the road within light scrub.

13. As the path (and the road) bears left, turn right to cross the road on the bend, with care, to a path opposite. Follow the path eastwards, passing Hodcombe Farm on the right to reach a path junction. Turn right and in 100 metres turn left and continue ahead from 5 (above).

South Downs National Park

2 SEVEN SISTERS COUNTRY PARK

A WALK ALONG THE RIVER CUCKMERE TO THE SEA FROM THE VISITOR CENTRE, AND THEN BEYOND THE COUNTRY PARK ONTO THE CLIFF TOPS OF THE SEVEN SISTERS AND TO THE HISTORIC HAMLET OF WESTDEAN.

The view from the Visitor Centre, and especially from the field at the rear of the Centre (on the way to Westdean), of the oxbows and the River Cuckmere to the sea at Cuckmere Haven is, in the opinion of the author, one of the finest in East Sussex. The number of visitors who make the journey and enjoy this walk, or a variation of it, supports this opinion.

Because of fears that the ease of access from the sea would make this area a target for an invasion during World War II, gun emplacements and pill boxes were constructed and can still be seen as the walk approaches the wide shingle beach. This is mostly man-made and a form of sea defence requiring regular maintenance. The cost of this maintenance has recently been questioned and many discussions and meetings have taken place to try to resolve the question of whether to continue maintaining the defences or to allow them to slowly break down, thus allowing the tide to inundate the Haven, the oxbows and the valley bottom up as far as the Visitor Centre every high tide.

Exceat Church was once high on the hill on the east side of the valley, just 50 metres off the South Downs Way route. The site is now marked with a stone bearing an inscription. The text claims the church was abandoned in the fifteenth century.

The walk along the iconic Seven Sisters chalk cliffs is one of the finest in Sussex, if not in all southern England. This walk offers a taster of the cliffs with a venture up from the Cuckmere Valley to the first of the Sisters.

Westdean is a hidden gem of a community lying deep in Friston Forest and only approached by a narrow lane or the footpath used during this walk (on the South Downs Way route). It consists of flint-built cottages, a Saxon church and a thirteenth-century rectory. The restored fourteenth-century flint dovecote is a credit to the owner, who completed the restoration himself in 2009. It is said that Alfred the Great had a palace in the village during his reign (871 to 899). Another claim made by the Old Parsonage is that it is the oldest continuously inhabited house in England. Others may dispute this claim.

Telephone boxes are a rare sight in this technological world, but two remain (although not in working order) on this walk. One sits opposite the Visitor Centre and the other opposite the pond in Westdean. They differ from the once familiar red phone boxes in that they are painted green.

THE BASICS

Distance: 4½ miles / 7.2km

Gradient: Gentle ascent/descent, longer steady ascent/descent and steep ascent/ descent and steps to Westdean

Severity: Moderate

Approx. time to walk: 3 to 3½ hours

Stiles: One 'wall' stile

Maps: OS Explorer 123 (Eastbourne and Beachy Head); OS Landranger 199 (Eastbourne and Hastings)

Path description: Riverbank and downland path and shingle beach, stepped woodland path and village lane

Start Point: Seven Sisters Country Park Visitor Centre (GR TV 519995)

Parking: Large car parks either side of A259 close to Visitor Centre (PC BN25 4AD)

Dog friendly: If they can manage stiles, and should be on leads

Public Toilets: At Visitor Centre

Nearest food: Tea rooms at rear of Visitor Centre; pub 600 metres west of Visitor Centre on A259

Look out for: Lullington Heath and Alfriston Clergy House (NT)

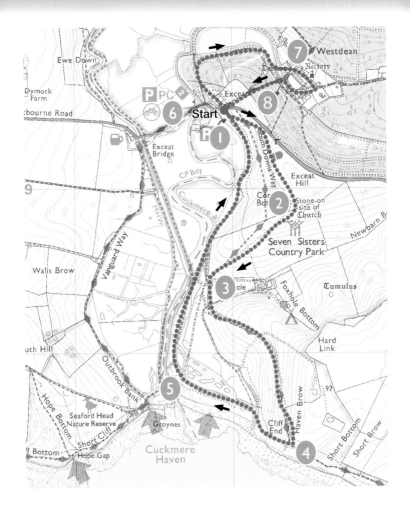

ROUTE

1. Cross the road from the Visitor Centre (with great care) and pass through the gateway on the concrete road.

2. In about 50 metres turn off left onto the grass path (the South Downs Way, SDW). The path ascends gently for about 500 metres to reach a gate into a field. The site of the former Exceat church is on the left, away from the path. Pass through the gate and follow the path bearing half-right and descending gently to another gate and return to the concrete road.

3. Turn left, remaining on the SDW. Pass through a gate and ascend gently to reach the top of the cliff at Haven Brow (the first of the Seven Sisters).

4. Take the steep path down to the beach at Cuckmere Haven.

5. Follow the concrete road and the river bank path to return to the Centre.

6. To visit Westdean, pass through the gate next to the cycle hire premises to rejoin the SDW. Enter a field and ascend steeply to the wall. Cross the wall, turn right and left into woodland and descend the steps down through the woodland to reach Westdean and pond on left.

7. Explore the hamlet of Westdean.

8. Return to the pond and take the track to the left of the pond into woodland. Follow the path through woodland as it bears left and left again to return to the rear of the Visitor Centre through car park.

South Downs National Park

3 WILMINGTON

THIS WALK TAKES IN THREE DOWNLAND VILLAGES, A SECTION
OF THE SOUTH DOWNS WAY AND A VISIT TO THE 'LONG MAN'
OF WILMINGTON.

Wilmington, the first of the three communities visited, is dominated by the giant chalk figure of the Long Man, just one of many chalk figures cut in the downlands of southern England. However, at over 70 metres tall the Long Man is one of the largest, and is one of only two human figures (the other being the Cerne Abbas giant in Dorset). For many years the origin of the chalk figure has baffled archaeologists and historians; the first recorded reference is a drawing dated to 1710, but he is believed to be older and probably dates from the sixteenth century. The figure has undergone several reconstructions and today is laid out with blocks painted white. During World War II the figure was painted green to hide what would be a useful navigational landmark for enemy aircraft.

Apart from the Long Man, Wilmington has a wonderful scattering of flint cottages, a twelfth century church, one of the oldest yew trees in Sussex and the remains of a priory. The Church of St Mary and St Peter was built next to the priory to serve the needs of both the village community and the occupants of the priory, with a covered cloister walk once connecting the two buildings. The North Chapel contains a beautiful window known as the

Bee and Butterfly window, depicting species seen locally. The ancient giant yew tree (with a girth of 23 feet) dominates the churchyard and is between 1,500 and 2,000 years old.

The village of Jevington was for forty-four years the home of the Hungry Monk restaurant. This has now closed, but its claim to fame was that it was the place where Banoffee Pie was created. A plaque celebrates the event.

On exiting north from the churchyard at St Andrew's Church you will encounter an unusual style of gate; this is a tapsell gate. There are six such gates in Sussex and the design is unique to the county. They pivot on a central post and are thought to offer coffin bearers easier access to the church.

Having entered Jevington on the South Downs Way, the walk leaves the village on the Wealdway. This 82-mile long-distance footpath crosses the south-east corner of England between the Sussex coast at Eastbourne and Gravesend in Kent.

Folkington is the final and smallest of the three communities. The walk passes St Peter's Church, and in the graveyard, can be found the grave of Elizabeth David OBE (1913–92), the British cookery writer. The tombstone is carved appropriately with a selection of vegetables and a cooking pot. Her father, James Gwynne, was MP for Eastbourne between 1910 and 1924, and the manor house was the family home for around a century. Two modern-day sculptures based on the Long Man can be seen in the woodland garden that lies behind the church.

THE BASICS

Distance: 6 miles / 9.5km

Gradient: One main ascent just after the start

Severity: Moderate

Approx. time to walk: 3 hours

Stiles: One

Maps: OS Explorer 123 (Eastbourne and Beachy Head); OS Landranger 199 (Eastbourne and Hastings)

Path description: Open downland paths and tracks, village lanes and woodland tracks

Start Point: Wilmington village car park (GR TQ 543042)

Parking: Free car park (PC BN26 5SW)

Dog friendly: If they can manage stiles and should be on leads

Public Toilets: None on route

Nearest food: The Giant's Rest pub in Wilmington; the Eight Bells pub in Jevington (on route)

Look out for: The Long Man of Wilmington and Michelham Priory (HHA)

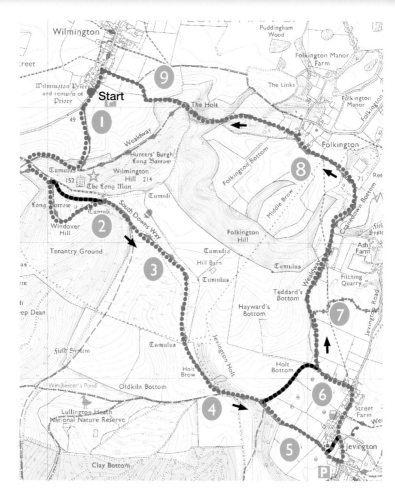

ROUTE

1. On leaving the car park, cross the road with care and turn right onto an enclosed path that runs parallel with the road for about 150 metres.

2. Turn left onto a bridle path and away from the road. The path gently ascends between hedges. Pass through a gate to reach cross-paths directly beneath the Long Man.

3. Turn right on an open downland path that bears to the left and ascends to another path junction.

Turn left on an ascending track that is joined by the South Downs Way (SDW) from the right. Continue ahead following the SDW, bearing right and left over Windover Hill.

4. Remain on the SDW over the hill and along a ridge until the track gradually descends through woodland.

5. Passing through a track junction, remain on the SDW, descending more steeply on an enclosed path towards the village of Jevington. Descend to the road and turn left through the village.

6. To visit the church, take the path on the left before reaching the road. Either return the same way or pass through the churchyard and along an enclosed path to the road. Turn left.

7. Walk through the village, pass the Eight Bells pub on the left and on nearing the end of the houses turn left onto a farm track. Continue on this wide track into light woodland for about 400 metres.

8. Turn right onto a bridle path (the Wealdway). Follow this rough track through light woodland and scrub for about 2 km to reach Folkington Church on the right with a small car park on the left.

9. To continue, remain on the undulating track through woodland before descending gently to emerge into open downland. The track crosses through fields to reach the lane at Wilmington opposite the church. Turn left to return to the car park.

4 SOUTHEASE & RODMELL

A CIRCULAR WALK IN THE HEART OF THE LOWER OUSE VALLEY, VISITING TWO SMALL ANCIENT COMMUNITIES LOCATED ON THE GENTLE WESTERN SLOPES OF THE VALLEY AND PASSING THE HOME OF WRITER VIRGINIA WOOLF ON THE WAY. THE WALK CAN BE STARTED FROM EITHER SOUTHEASE OR RODMELL (DESCRIBED BELOW), OR ALTERNATIVELY FROM SOUTHEASE RAILWAY STATION, THE LATTER OPTION ADDING HALF A MILE TO THE DISTANCE WALKED.

Rodmell is the larger of the two communities and straddles the busy Newhaven Road between Lewes and Newhaven. The Abergavenny Arms dominates the village at this point. On the opposite side of the road the village blacksmith and farrier has been in the same family for over a century. A walk east away from the pub takes you gently through the older part of the village, passing many houses that date from centuries past.

St Peter's Church in Rodmell lies directly behind Monk's House, now in the hands of the National Trust but once the home of Virginia Woolf, until the fateful day in 1941 when she walked down to the river and drowned herself. Her husband Leonard continued to live in the village until 1969.

The lane leads away from the village and across the now drained flood plain to the banks of the River Ouse. Southease Bridge was fully restored in 2010 at a cost of £1.7 million. Originally built in the late eighteenth century, the bridge was constructed with a centre section that could swing open to allow larger vessels to sail upriver to Lewes. By the 1980s this was no longer a requirement and the latest restoration did not repair the swing mechanism.

It is hard to believe that Southease village once had a flourishing herring fishing industry. The village green is dominated by the church, one of just three round-towered churches in Sussex, all in the Ouse valley. Walkers undertaking the South Downs Way National Trail contribute greatly to the foot traffic passing through this otherwise tranquil village.

THE BASICS

Distance: 3 miles / 5km (3¾ miles / 6km if choosing the Southease Station start/ finish)

Gradient: Mainly flat, one gentle ascent

Severity: Easy

Approx. time to walk: 2 – 2½ hours

Stiles: One

Maps: OS Explorer 122 (Brighton and Hove);
OS Landranger 198 (Brighton and Lewes)

Path description: Village lanes, tracks, riverbank path, field edge

Start Point: Newhaven Road, Rodmell (GR TQ 418059)

Parking: Limited street parking. Abergavenny Arms has parking (please seek permission; PC BN7 3EZ)

Dog friendly: If they can manage stiles and should be on leads

Public Toilets: None (please seek permission in Abergavenny Arms)

Nearest food: Abergavenny Arms; Youth Hostel (opened 2013) next to Itford Farm on A26 east of Southease Station (GR TQ 433055)

Look out for: Monk's House (NT), Breaky Bottom Vineyard

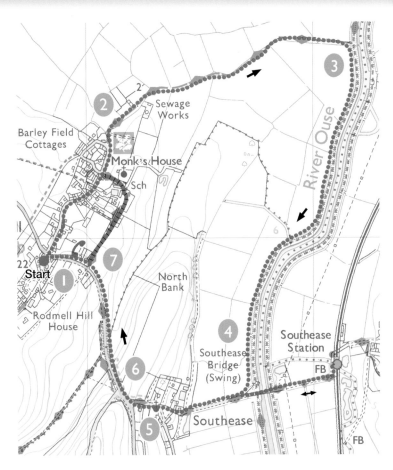

ROUTE

1. Walk away from the main road and the Abergavenny Arms eastwards gently downhill on the lane, passing through the houses of Rodmell. In 500 metres, reach Monk's House on the right. Immediately before then, turn right into a narrow lane to view Rodmell Church.

2. Continue along the lane, which becomes a rough track upon leaving the village. Pass through gates as the route emerges out into open fields to cross the drainage ditches of the river flood plain.

3. Reach the high riverbanks of the River Ouse. Ascend onto the footpath on the bank and turn right (south).

4. Follow the riverbank for about 1 mile to reach Southease Bridge. Those starting and finishing the walk at Southease Station (400 metres east) should join/leave the route at this point. Turn right onto a tarmac lane.

5. Reach Southease village green. Continue ahead uphill, passing the church on the left. In 50 metres turn right, after passing a cottage on the right, through a gateway. Immediately turn left through another gate onto an enclosed path. The path was recently laid down following an agreement with landowners and the residents of the villages to allow for a safe and improved route between their communities.

6. Follow this path around the edge of the field, then descend steps to continue on the path with a tree line on the left shielding the road.

7. Reach a rough track that emerges onto the road on the left. Turn left and then right onto the pavement to walk back into Rodmell and the starting point. (Turn right and follow the track to reach a path into the rear of Rodmell Church.)

5 FIRLE AND ALCISTON

A WALK THAT EXPLORES TWO OF THE ANCIENT AND PICTURESQUE DOWNLAND VILLAGE COMMUNITIES THAT NESTLE BELOW THE SOUTH DOWNS SCARP FACE. IT ALSO PASSES CHARLESTON FARMHOUSE, ONCE THE COUNTRY RETREAT OF THE BLOOMSBURY SET. THE WALK COULD BE STARTED FROM EITHER OF THE VILLAGES.

West Firle retains an air of days gone by, and it is mentioned in the Domesday survey of 1086. The Church of St Peter dates from the thirteenth century or earlier, and at the time of writing the village still boasts a village shop and pub, essentials of community life that many other villages struggle to hold on to in the twenty-first century.

The Firle Estate came into the Gage family in the fifteenth century and remains with the family to this day. The building of Firle Place began in 1557. This grand home is open to the public during the summer months and houses a wealth of fine paintings, furniture and porcelain. Firle Tower becomes visible after leaving Firle. It is a substantial building with glazed windows, offering fine views of the Estate. It was built as a lookout and also served as accommodation for gamekeepers.

Charleston Farmhouse is not noted for its architectural importance but for being the retreat of the Bloomsbury Set. From 1916 the farmhouse was home to Vanessa Bell (Virginia Woolf's sister), Duncan Grant and her children, and it became the meeting place of many artists and writers from the London literary scene. The house is decorated throughout in the distinctive style associated with those within the Set. It is open to the public and attracts thousands of visitors each year.

Alciston is the second of the villages; picturesque cottages line the street and the medieval dovecote (once believed to house seven hundred nest boxes) situated close to the church is a particular attraction. The village is dominated at its southern end by the sixteenth-century Great Barn, at 170 feet (52 metres) one of the longest tithe barns in Sussex.

The Old Coach Road, followed for about 2 miles on this walk, is the former route taken by the horse-drawn coaches along the scarp face of the Downs before the modern-day A27 was completed. Be warned that the old track suffers from muddy conditions during wet weather.

THE BASICS

Distance: 6 miles / 10km

Gradient: Level walking, no hills

Severity: Easy

Approx. time to walk: 3 hours

Stiles: Two

Maps: OS Explorer 123 (Eastbourne and Beachy Head); OS Landranger 198 (Brighton and Lewes)

Path description: Tracks, field paths and village lanes. May be muddy when wet

Start Point: West Firle village (GR TQ 470072)

Parking: Limited street parking in village (PC BN8 6NY)

Dog friendly: If they can manage stiles and should be on leads

Public Toilets: At Charleston Farmhouse (when house is open) and at pubs on route

Nearest food: The Rose Cottage Inn at Alciston and the Ram at West Firle

Look out for: Firle Beacon, Firle Place and Charleston Farmhouse

5 FIRLE AND ALCISTON WALK

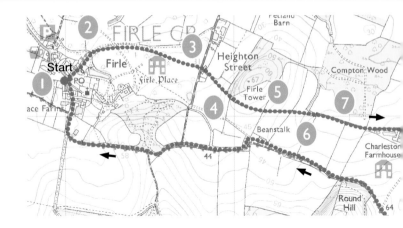

ROUTE

1. From the church gate opposite the village shop, turn right into a narrow lane with a high wall on the right and cottages on the left. At the end of the lane reach a gateway into the Firle Estate.

2. Within the estate, turn half-right off a rough track across grassland. Cross the main drive at a signpost and continue ahead across the grassland following a line of low posts. Firle Place lies to the right.

3. Reach a gateway and emerge onto a lane opposite a house. Cross the lane and pass between the houses to a metal gateway onto a field path. Within 20 metres the path bears to the right of a flint wall into a field. Follow the wall on a path that ascends to woodland.

4. Upon reaching the woodland turn right for about 25 metres. Turn left through a gap to a track with a gate on the left.

5. Cross the track and pass through a hedge gap into a field. Continue ahead across the field with Firle Tower now on the left horizon.

6. Pass through a gap into another field and continue ahead into a third field. Head half-left towards a band of trees, cross a ditch and a watercourse and turn right to the corner of the field and a gate on the left into another field.

7. In 5 metres turn right and follow the right-hand field boundary towards Charleston Farmhouse. Two more sets of gates lead to the farm with car park and main farmhouse on left, toilets on right.

8. Continue on the concrete drive, and when the drive turns left after 150 metres cross to a gate into a field.

9. Follow the right-hand field boundary, with Tilton Farm on the right. Pass through a tree line and a gate into another field and continue ahead to a gate at the corner of the woodland. In the next field the path ascends slightly (Mill Hill) with woodland on the right to reach 'Keepers', a cottage that is home to the Sarah Walton Pottery, on the right and a concrete drive.

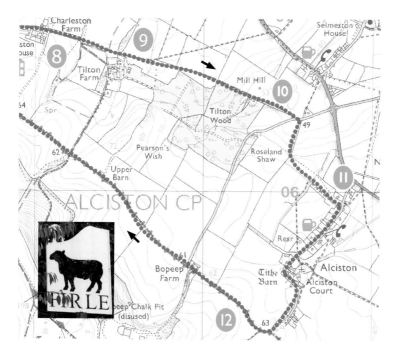

10. At the end of the drive reach a lane. Turn left and in about 20 metres turn right over a stile into a field. Walk down the left-hand field boundary to a gate into another field. Ascend on the right-hand boundary to the field corner and turn left. Continue along

the boundary to kissing gates and a small footbridge over a watercourse into another field. Cross towards houses and pass through a gate to the road at Alciston.

11. Turn right along the road, passing the Rose Cottage Inn. Continue through the village passing the Great Barn. The road bears right and ends as it meets with the Old Coach Road.

12. Turn right and follow the track for about 2.5 miles to return to the village of West Firle.

6 LEWES AND THE CABURN

A CHALLENGING DOWNLAND WALK OUT OF LEWES ONTO
MALLING DOWN, AN IMPORTANT NATURE RESERVE, AND THE
CABURN, AN IRON AGE HILLFORT OFFERING SPECTACULAR
VIEWS DOWN THE OUSE VALLEY AND ACROSS THE WEALD.

The steep start to this walk offers views back over Lewes. The green-painted building below is the Snowdrop Inn. In 1837 a snowfall engulfed the buildings below, resulting in eight deaths.

At 490 feet (150 metres) the Caburn dominates the Ouse Valley on the approach to Lewes and hovers over the Glynde Reach, the river that rises further east near Heathfield and flows into the Ouse further downstream. The Caburn is the site of an Iron Age hillfort. Its prominent position above the Ouse Valley allows views of the River Ouse as it reaches out to the English Channel, although unlike today the sea would once have come further up the valley. There is evidence that this important vantage point has been used during many of the conflicts that have threatened our country over the centuries.

Low marker stones seen in the ground along the path approaching the golf course indicate where the ancient boundaries of the local parishes of Ringmer, Glynde and Malling met. The Martyrs' Memorial, shown as 'obelisk' on the OS map, was erected in 1901. It commemorates the seventeen Protestant martyrs who were burned to death for their faith between the years of 1555 and 1557 outside what is now the Town Hall in Lewes during the reign of Queen Mary I.

The Malling Down Nature Reserve is managed by the Sussex Wildlife Trust. The aim is to preserve the grassland as it was in the days when large flocks of sheep were on the Downs. The grazing sheep kept the invasive scrub at bay and created the downland turf. Sheep are back on Malling Down, but not in the numbers of days gone by. Look out for the Herdwick breed, more commonly seen on the fells of the Lake District but ideally suited to the exposed slopes of the Downs. The round-headed rampion, the flower known as the Pride of Sussex, can also be seen.

The Cuilfail Tunnel carries road traffic away from the town centre and passes beneath Chapel Hill at the start and finish of the walk. It is named after the Cuilfail Estate which lies beyond the obelisk, perched on the edge of the hill. The estate was developed by Isaac Vinall, who named it after his favourite Scottish hill.

THE BASICS

Distance: 4½ miles / 7.2km

Gradient: Steep ascent at start, undulating downland, steep descent at finish

Severity: Hard

Approx. time to walk: 2½ hours

Stiles: None

Maps: OS Explorer 122 (Brighton and Hove); OS Landranger 198 (Brighton and Lewes)

Path description: Town lane, downland and golf course paths

Start Point: Phoenix Causeway car park, Lewes (GR TQ 422103)

Parking: Various car parking in Lewes town (payment required) (PC BN7 2JW and BN7 2LE)

Dog friendly: On leads

Public Toilets: In car park off Friars Walk (200 metres from start)

Nearest food: Various food outlets in Lewes town

Look out for: Glynde Place (HHA), and in Lewes, Lewes Castle and Museum. Historical houses include Anne of Cleves' house.

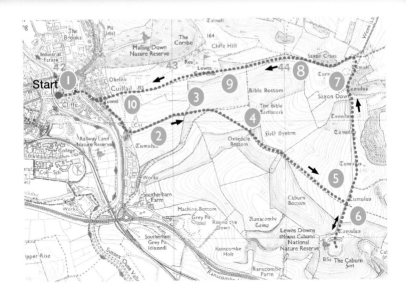

ROUTE

1. Walk from the car park along Cliffe High Street away from Cliffe Bridge to the junction with South Street and Malling Street. Cross the junction into Chapel Hill. The lane ascends steeply, and after about 600 metres reaches the golf clubhouse on the left.

2. Turn right at the fingerpost into a narrow path along the right edge of the car park for 20 metres to reach a gate. Pass through the gate and turn left, following a fence until you emerge into open downland.

3. Continue ahead on a wide path. On reaching a marker post bear half-right, descend, and in 100 metres reach a gate. Follow the path, descending gradually to another gate and fingerpost. Pass through the gate and continue diagonally left across the open land, following marker posts to reach the bottom of the valley and farm gates.

4. Turn right through the gates and pass a dewpond on the left. Continue ahead on a path close to a wire fence along the right-hand field boundary to reach the corner of the field. Just left of the corner, by an English Nature noticeboard, cross a stile.

Continue ahead on a wide, ascending path, bearing away from the right-hand boundary fence. Reach another stile in the fence line at the top of the hill.

5. Turn right and follow the path, passing through two kissing gates to reach the Caburn.

6. Retrace your steps from the Caburn through the kissing gates and continue ahead, passing the stile previously crossed on the left, and follow the left-hand fence line. Pass through a farm gate, or cross the stile, to continue across open land to another farm gate. Pass through and bear half-left onto a grass track for 25 metres.

7. Cross a track junction onto a grass track which gradually ascends over a hill. Remain on the path, which bears slightly right towards the corner of the fence line and a boundary stone.

8. Pass to the right of the corner and follow the path with the fence on your left to reach a farm gate. Pass through and ascend towards the golf course. About halfway up the hill reach a boundary stone on the right, where the path divides.

9. Take the left fork and follow the path in a direct line across the golf course.

10. On the far side of the golf course with the obelisk on the right, continue ahead to reach Chapel Hill. Turn right and return to the start.

iStock

7 STANMER & DITCHLING BEACON

A SLIGHTLY CHALLENGING WALK THAT ASCENDS OUT OF STANMER PARK ONTO THE SOUTH DOWNS WAY RIDGE OVER OPEN DOWNLAND TO THE HEIGHTS OF DITCHLING BEACON. THE RETURN IS A MORE GENTLE DESCENT ACROSS DOWNLAND WITH WIDE VIEWS ACROSS THE CITY OF BRIGHTON.

The ancient village of Stanmer lies within Stanmer Park on the outskirts of Brighton. Adjacent to the park is the University of Sussex campus. The village dates back over a thousand years and for centuries it belonged to the church until the dissolution of the monasteries during the reign of Henry VIII.

A church has stood on the edge of the village since the thirteenth century, although the present-day building is mainly Victorian. In 2008 the Diocese of Chichester declared the church redundant with no regular services taking place. However, the Stanmer Preservation Society now maintains the Grade II listed building. They keep it open on Sundays and for other special events and concerts. The churchyard contains a rare well-house with a donkey wheel which is also Grade II listed. The donkey wheel dates from at least the eighteenth century and is also maintained by the Stanmer Preservation Society. The Society was formed in 1971 and is a charity committed to improving, protecting and preserving the Estate.

The Grade I-listed Stanmer House dominates the park and the approach to the village. The original house was built in 1722 by the French architect Nicholas Dubois for the Pelham family of Lewes. They were associated with the village, and in 1713 Henry Pelham bought the whole estate for £7,500. His son, also Henry, built the first house here, which was later incorporated in extensive nineteenth-century alterations. The estate remained in the Pelham family until World War II, when the house was requisitioned by the War Office until 1946. It was then purchased by Brighton Corporation when the Pelhams' finances were badly hit by inheritance taxes. Between 1969 and 1980 it became part of Sussex University and was used as administration offices. After 1980 the house was neglected, but in 2004 it was saved by private investors and today it is a successful conference, dining and function centre.

At 814 feet (248 metres), Ditchling Beacon is one of the highest points on the South Downs. The view north across Sussex is a great reward for the effort made during the steady ascent from Stanmer. The village of Ditchling lies below the Beacon a mile to the north.

THE BASICS

Distance: 5¼ miles / 8.5km

Gradient: Gradual and then steeper ascent from start to Beacon

Severity: Moderate

Approx. time to walk: 2½ to 3 hours

Stiles: Two

Maps: OS Explorer 122 (Brighton and Hove); OS Landranger 198 (Brighton and Lewes)

Path description: Village roads, tracks, grass downland

Start Point: Stanmer village centre/church (GR TQ 337096)

Parking: Free car parks in Stanmer Park (PC BN1 9PZ)

Dog friendly: If they can manage stiles and should be on leads

Public Toilets: In Stanmer village just after start of walk

Nearest food: Tea rooms in Stanmer village

Look out for: Ditchling Beacon (NT) and Castle Hill nature reserve (NT)

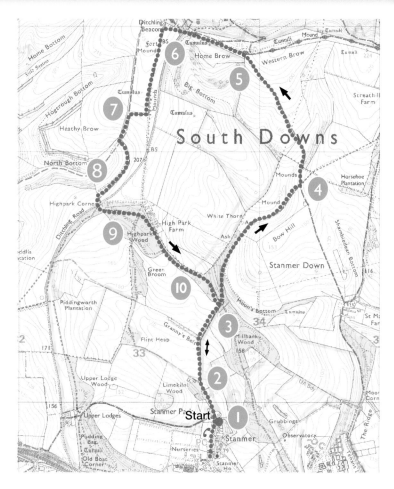

ROUTE

Explore the village and the area around the church and Stanmer House before or after the walk.

1. Walk away from the car park and church along the lane, passing the tea rooms and toilets and through the houses and farm buildings of the village.

2. At the end of the village lane reach a gate. Pass through the gate onto a track, gradually ascending onto open downland.

3. The track ascends to a track junction at the top of the ascent. Bear right into woodland on this track.

4. Follow the track through the woodland until it emerges through a gateway into open land again. Remain on the field path that ascends again to cross-tracks. Turn left on the bridleway.

5. Follow the path ascending steeply for about 1 kilometre to meet the South Downs Way (SDW). Turn left onto the SDW.

6. Reach the roadway opposite Ditchling Beacon car park. Cross the road with great care and pass to the right of the car park, still on the SDW. The path ascends briefly to reach the top of the Beacon with the triangulation point on the left.

7. As the path descends away from the Beacon take the footpath on the left. The path runs parallel with the road for about 750 metres then turns right to meet another path. Turn left.

8. Follow this path for about 200 metres. Turn left on a path that bears right and continues south, following the line of the road to emerge onto the road.

9. Cross with care to a path and a junction. Bear left on a path through a wooded area and pass a farm on the left (High Park Farm). The path continues through a wooded tree line to return to the path junction (point 3 above).

10. Turn right and return to Stanmer village.

8 HURSTPIERPOINT

This walk introduces you to many old Sussex names. The name Hurstpierpoint comes from the Old English 'herst', a wooded hill, and Pierre Pont, the family name of the Norman baron who was given lands here after the Norman Conquest. The village sign is a copy of the effigy of Simon de Pierre Pont found in the church. He was the last member of that family to live here and died in 1343.

Coldharbour is a common placename in Sussex and there are many debates as to its meaning. It has been associated with Roman roads, inland river transport and ancient boundaries. One likely meaning is a place of sanctuary or shelter.

Watch out for the alpacas and llamas on the Danny Estate! Both come from the high Andes and are closely related, but alpacas are smaller and are bred for their fleece while llamas are generally used as pack animals. Sheep also graze the Danny estate and their spring lambs are protected from foxes by two llamas. Alpacas were found not to be good guards but the llamas have successfully earned their keep.

The name Danny is a corruption of the Saxon Danehithe, meaning 'valley and haven'. There has been a house on this site since the thirteenth century. Originally a hunting lodge for the medieval deer park, the current house was built during the reign of Queen Elizabeth

I by George Goring. The house has many historical links. In 1918 it was rented for Prime Minister David Lloyd George, and it was here that a meeting of the Imperial War Cabinet agreed that a cable should be sent to the US President Wilson authorising him to proceed with negotiations for an armistice with Germany. The house is now privately owned and run as serviced apartments for retired people.

Bedlam is another common placename, and not just in Sussex. Derived from 'Bethlehem' – 'house of bread' – it was originally the name for a hospital for the sick or indigent poor, but it was later shortened to Bedlam and came to mean a lunatic asylum. There was probably such a place on Bedlam Street.

THE BASICS

Distance: 5¼ miles / 8.4km

Gradient: Gently rolling countryside with very few gradients

Severity: Easy terrain, with lots of stiles and some careful navigation required

Approx. time to walk: 2¼ hours

Stiles: Eighteen

Maps: OS Explorer 122 (Brighton and Hove); OS Landranger 198 (Brighton and Lewes)

Path description: Mostly open parkland

Start Point: Trinity Road car park, Hurstpierpoint (GR TQ 281165)

Parking: Free disc parking (PC BN6 9UY)*

Dog friendly: If they can manage the stiles, and should be on leads because of sheep in the fields around Danny

Public Toilets: Beside the car park

Nearest food: Vineyard Lodge restaurant/bar or the New Inn

Look out for: The All England Jumping Course at Hickstead, and Clayton Tunnel (castle built at the entrance to a railway tunnel, PC BN6 9PD)

* Parking discs can be purchased for a £1 administration charge from the leisure centres or at several local retailers. Please see the signs displayed within the car parks for further details

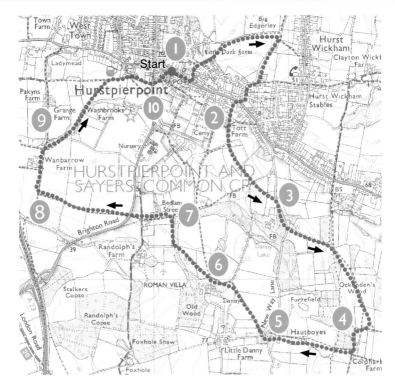

ROUTE

1. From the car park walk towards the library and turn right. Cross the brow of a hill, and opposite the Health Centre take the footpath sign left. Enter a large field and swing around the northern edge, before meeting a crossing footpath in the woods. Here, turn right. Walk ahead as the path  opens out to become St George's Lane; pass the disused church and on reaching the main road turn right for 30 metres then cross carefully to climb steps into the woods opposite.

2. This path leads over two stiles down a grassy bank to a tarmac drive. Follow the lane straight ahead towards the downs, passing The Granary on your right. Pass through a metal gate to a farm track. After a couple of gates and 'pinch-points' the path goes straight over a tarmac drive, up a small hill and over two stiles to reach a public road.

3. Turn right heading downhill, and at a house called Bearstakes turn left to follow the hedge left over three stiles to reach a crossing footpath. Turn right through a kissing gate. Cross the next field diagonally heading towards Jack and Jill Windmills in the distance. After two more kissing gates take the right fork, and at the far side of the field cross a pinch-point into the woods.

4. Turn right then left to reach Coldharbour Farm and turn right over a stile besides a gate. After one more stile and two pinch-points reach Hautboyes; walk past the house on the outside of their fence and then enter the drive through a pinch-point.

5. At the end of the drive turn left on the tarmac road, and in 20 metres turn right following the footpath fingerpost into the woods. A plank bridge and stile lead into an open field where you may see the alpacas on either side. Two more stiles lead onto the drive at the entrance to the splendid house called Danny. Cross straight over the drive to pass just north of the house.

6. Just before the outbuildings a footpath fingerpost leads over a stile to the right. A further stile, plank bridge and pinch-point lead into an open field where the path forks across the field. Take the left fork, heading just left of two large trees. Two more stiles lead into the next field, at the far side of which you enter the woods over a stile. Exit over another stile to walk around the edge of a large paddock.

7. At the next crossing footpath turn left, and the path soon becomes a driveway passing through the tile-hung houses of Bedlam Street. The driveway (from Randolphs Farm) becomes tarmac and in 100 metres reaches the main road. Cross carefully and follow the footpath on the far side for 300 metres to pass through a big gap in the hedge line. Continue along the edges of two more fields to reach a crossing footpath.

8. Turn right to head north. Just after the outbuildings of Wanbarrow Farm, reach a crossroads of paths and turn right on a wide track to leave a large open field on your right. Take care now, because in just 200 metres the footpath forks left away from the main track onto a grassy path into the trees.

9. Cross a footbridge over a stream and then follow the stream to a kissing gate, after which the path heads in the general direction of Hurstpierpoint Church, passing through two more kissing gates before reaching a four-armed fingerpost. Take the bridleway going slightly right to pass just south of the church and reach the main road.

10. Cross carefully to the path opposite and in 50 metres, at the next footpath junction, turn left along West Furlong Lane to the High Street where a quick left and right turn will lead you back into the car park.

9 STEYNING

Steyning is a medieval market town with a recorded history going back over a thousand years. The town's founding father was St Cuthman, who, after the death of his father in Wessex around AD 700, brought his ageing mother here in what resembled a wheelbarrow. When he reached this piece of high ground between two streams the ropes holding the barrow broke, and he took this as a sign from God that he should settle here and build a church.

You will see his statue as you leave the car park. It depicts him as a builder looking towards where his church stood. His original wooden building was replaced by the much larger St Andrew's Church we see today, constructed a mere 850 years ago. If the church is open do take a look.

As you walk up Church Street, even a cursory glance at the buildings shows how much history there is here. On your right is The Forge, where Charles II rested on 14 October 1651 while his companion, Colonel Gunter, had his horse re-shod. Little did they realise that Cromwell had troops based in Bramber less than a mile away.

The Memorial Playing Fields provide fine views of the downs and Chanctonbury Ring in the distance. Much of the rural part of this walk falls within the Steyning Downland Scheme; 160 acres of chalk downland have been designated for the benefit of wildlife and the local community, and are known locally as the Horseshoe and the Rifle Range.

As you return to town you cross the millstream and get a brief glimpse of the old wheel. Court Mill produced animal feed, but closed in 1927. The road from here down to the High Street is Sir George's Place, named after George Breach who founded a tannery here in 1820 and built these houses for his workers. He was never knighted but was so popular that everyone called him 'Sir George'. During the First World War many of the sheepskin jerkins worn by our troops were made at his tannery.

On the High Street there are many buildings to admire but one of the most noticeable is the clock tower beneath which is Old Market House, where George Fox, a founder of the Society of Friends (Quakers), held a meeting in 1655. It has been at various times the Town Hall, a Police Station and a Fire Station. The clock itself was a gift from the Duke of Norfolk and was put up in 1860, although the building itself is much older.

THE BASICS

Distance: 2¼ miles / 3.5km

Gradient: One very gentle climb and descent

Severity: Easy

Approx. time to walk: 1 hour

Stiles: None

Maps: OS Explorer 121 (Arundel and Pulborough) and 122 (Brighton and Hove); OS Landranger 198 (Brighton and Lewes)

Path description: Parkland, good footpaths and road surfaces

Start Point: Opposite St Andrews Church, Steyning (GR TQ 179113)

Parking: Fletchers Croft car park opposite St Andrews Church (PC BN44 3XZ)

Dog friendly: On leads in the town

Public Toilets: By the Steyning Centre in the car park and in the High Street

Nearest food: Loads to choose from in the High Street

Look out for: Steyning Museum and independent shops

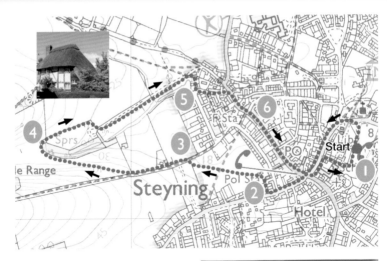

ROUTE

1. From Fletchers Croft car park, walk back towards the church and turn left along Church Street. On reaching the High Street cross straight over and walk past the White Horse Inn to reach White Horse Square, and turn right into Charlton Street.

2. In just 30 metres turn left by the police station onto the Memorial Playing Field. Cross the field, past the children's play area, to the far right-hand corner and exit through a kissing gate onto a rough track.

3. Turn left heading uphill and in 200 metres reach a second kissing gate and turn right through a third gate into an open area called Butterfly Land. Follow the clear grassy path ahead, which starts off level and then descends into the valley.

4. At the bottom follow the path right around the trees to almost reverse

direction and head back towards town. The grassy path gives way to a hard surface between elder and blackberry bushes, and nearing the town passes through a wooden gate. Immediately after this, and before reaching the thatched cottage, turn right on a narrower path through the bushes. As you cross the course of the old millstream there are views of Court Mill, with its old waterwheel, to the right.

5. On reaching the public road ahead turn left downhill, passing Sir George's Place to reach the Star Inn.

6. Turn right and walk up the High Street, admiring the many different timber-framed buildings in this medieval town, and return to the crossroads by the White Horse Inn. Turn left along Church Street and this time, opposite the Norfolk Arms, turn right down a passageway to return to the car park.

10 WASHINGTON

THE NAME OF WASHINGTON IS DERIVED FROM OLD ENGLISH, MEANING 'THE ESTATE OF THE FAMILY OR FOLLOWERS OF A MAN CALLED WASSA', AND WAS FIRST RECORDED IN AD 957. THE VILLAGE GREW UP AT THE CROSSING OF TWO MAIN ROUTES, ONE FOLLOWING AN EAST-WEST RIDGE AND THE OTHER RUNNING NORTH-SOUTH BETWEEN LONDON AND WORTHING.

In the late nineteenth century there were many stores and businesses serving the local population; in the 1920s three tearooms catered for increasing numbers of visitors arising from the growth of tourism by motor car. Sadly they have all long since closed. However, Washington has benefitted from local community action, and it now has a small shop beside the pub and teas are served at weekends in the village hall.

The memorial at the entrance to Sullington churchyard commemorates four local men who died in action during the First World War and the crew of submarine E24, which was sunk by a mine off Heligoland in March 1916. Lt Cd. Napier, captain of the E24, was a Sullington man.

Many ancient paths cross the downs here. 'Bostal' is a Sussex name for a narrow, winding track, usually climbing a steep north-facing escarpment. Just south of here were many flint mines that are believed by many to be the last home of fairies in England.

At the top of the downs the walk follows a section of the South Downs Way back down into Washington, crossing the busy A24 on a farm bridge. On the downs beyond the A24 can be seen the distinctive Chanctonbury Ring, an Iron Age hill fort where the remains of a Roman temple have also been found. The ring is visible for many miles and beacons were placed there to warn of possible invasions during the time of the Spanish Armada and the Napoleonic Wars.

Charles Goring planted the beech trees around the ring in 1760. There was a public outcry, as local people feared the line of the beautiful downs would be spoilt for future generations. However, the trees have become a landmark and their devastation in the storm of 1987 was greatly regretted. They are now beginning to recover.

THE BASICS

Distance: 4½ miles / 7.2km

Gradient: One long, easy ascent and one slightly steeper descent

Severity: Moderate

Approx. time to walk: 2 hours

Stiles: None

Maps: OS Explorer 121 (Arundel and Pulborough); OS Landranger 197 (Chichester and the South Downs) and 198 (Brighton and Lewes)

Path description: Mostly broad bostal tracks; one muddy section in wet weather

Start Point: Frankland Arms Inn, Washington (GR TQ 122129)

Parking: Unrestricted roadside parking (PC RH20 4AL)

Dog friendly: Cattle and sheep may be present on the downland section – keep dogs on leads

Public Toilets: Only at the inn

Nearest food: The Frankland Arms, Washington

Look out for: Chanctonbury Ring

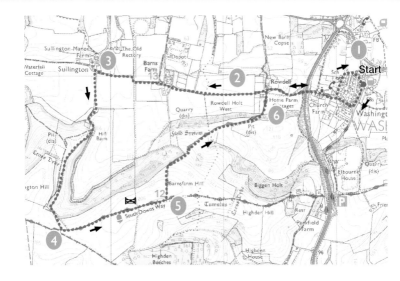

ROUTE

1. With your back to the inn turn right and walk along the road for 200 metres, then turn right into The Street. After passing St Mary's Church, cross the busy A24 on the road bridge and at the next fork keep right. In 100 metres, on reaching the first house, turn left into the trees and then almost immediately right following a blue bridleway sign.

2. Follow this path left then right as it emerges into open fields with fine views of the South Downs ahead to your left. The path goes around Barns Farm; at the far side, turn left to continue westwards on a more confined path between trees. At the end of this tree line take care as you cross the gallops, then continue in the same direction along the side of an open field to reach Sullington Manor Farm.

3. Turn right to visit the lovely church in its peaceful and picturesque setting. Now retrace your steps to where you entered the farmyard and head directly south towards the downs on a broad track. This briefly becomes concreted and climbs

quite steeply before passing a low farm building, after which the gradient eases into a typical downland bostal.

4. At the crest of the downs, just east of a hay barn, meet the South Downs Way and turn left to follow it. After crossing the brow of the next hill the trail begins its slow descent back towards Washington and soon passes through a metal gate. Just 250 metres after this gate, look for a turning to the left off the main trail to follow the alternative route avoiding the A24.

5. Turn left here and initially climb over a rise and pass a clump of bushes before beginning a long curving descent north-eastwards (take care that you are following the bridleway and not a wide farm track as you pass the bushes).

6. Near the foot of the downs the path enters trees and turns north to pass beside The Old Pump House and reach a crossroad of tracks. Continue ahead into the trees and in 25 metres, at the T-junction, turn right to retrace the steps of your outbound route. After again passing St Mary's Church take the first road left and walk quite steeply down School Lane, past the village hall and playing fields to emerge beside the garden of the Frankland Arms.

THE NAME OF THIS PRETTY VILLAGE DERIVES FROM TWO OLD ENGLISH WORDS, 'HAM' AND 'BURGH', WHICH ALSO – IN THAT ORDER – SPELL THE NAME OF A MUCH LARGER TOWN IN GERMANY! IT SIMPLY MEANS 'FORTIFIED SETTLEMENT', REFERRING TO THE ORIGINAL DEFENSIVE EARTHWORKS BUILT AROUND AD 900 TO GUARD AGAINST VIKING RAIDERS PLUNDERING THEIR WAY UP THE VALLEY. YOU'LL ENCOUNTER THE EARTHWORKS OF THE FORT AT THE END OF THE WALK AS YOU CLIMB UP FROM SPLASH FARM.

The village originally grew up within the Saxon fort but by the early Norman period it had moved to the northern entrance where the eleventh-century St Mary's Church was constructed. An unusual feature in the chancel is the lepers' window. The low window allowed lepers from the nearby colony, at what is now Lee Farm, to view the service without coming into contact with others. The track along Coombe Lane is the route they took to and from church and is known as Lepers Way.

For hundreds of years the River Arun provided a means of communication for the village, but with the cutting of a new river channel by the railway company in the 1860s the Burpham Loop, as it was known, became a backwater and the village wharf closed in 1887.

This walk is mostly through delightfully quiet and remote countryside, much of which was acquired by the Norfolk Estate at the end of the eighteenth century. The unspoilt nature of the area has attracted its fair share of writers and artists, the most well known being John Cooper Powys, Mervyn Peake and 'beekeeper' Tickner Edwardes, who features in the Arun Valley walk.

The inn at the end of the walk was for many years called the George and Dragon. The name was shortened in 2013 when it was acquired by a group of the local villagers, who now manage it very much as a communal centre with a small shop selling local produce.

THE BASICS

Distance: 3½ miles / 5.5km

Gradient: Short, easy ascent and a flight of steps; steeper road section downhill

Severity: Easy/moderate

Approx. time to walk: 1¾ hours

Stiles: Six

Maps: OS Explorer 121 (Arundel and Pulborough); OS Landranger 197 (Chichester and the South Downs)

Path description: Wide bostal (downland path) and grassy tracks with some quiet country lanes

Start Point: The George Inn, Burpham (GR TQ 039089)

Parking: Free public car park behind the George Inn (PC BN18 9RR)

Dog friendly: If they can manage the stiles, and should be on leads because of sheep on the downland section

Public Toilets: Only at the inn

Nearest food: The George Inn, Burpham

Look out for: Amberley Museum and Heritage Centre

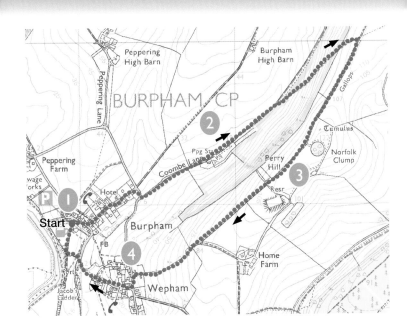

ROUTE

1. From the car park, walk back towards the George Inn and turn right. Keep left at the first fork in the road and continue ahead past Burpham Country House Hotel to a road junction. Turn right downhill and in 75 metres take the first bridleway left along Coombe Lane.

2. Walk past a house and water station to reach a wooden gate. Soon afterwards turn right, following the yellow footpath sign on a grassy path heading upwards to the horizon. Near the top of this rise, cross a stile beside a gate and continue straight ahead to join a much broader crossing path. Turn right.

3. As you pass a large clump of trees on your left the path becomes grassy and continues ahead with fine views of the Isle of Wight in the distance. After passing through a metal gate, begin descending gently downhill as Arundel Castle comes into view further down the valley. On reaching the next junction of paths cross a stile and turn half-right, heading more steeply downhill. The path immediately swings left and crosses two more stiles before reaching the public road.

4. Turn left, and in just 50 metres take the first road right, heading steeply downhill towards Splash Farm. Cross the ford on the raised path and take the path ahead, going up wooden steps on the side of the hill through the trees. At the top, cross two more stiles across an open field and turn right past the children's playground to the car park behind the George Inn.

12 ARUN VALLEY

This walk becomes circular by dint of a five-minute train journey from Amberley Station back to the start point in Arundel Station. The train runs at least hourly, there is a choice of excellent refreshments while you wait, and provided you stay on the east platform (do not cross the footbridge over the line), every train that stops will also stop at Arundel – just one station down the line. It's perhaps a good idea before you set out to check on return train times from Amberley. You can find these on the website www.nationalrail.co.uk.

Soon after the Norman Conquest of 1066, William I ordered the building of castles to defend his new realm. Those along the south coast included Lewes, Bramber and Arundel, which protected the estuaries of the three major Sussex rivers – the Ouse, Adur and Arun.

This walk explores the valley of the River Arun as it cuts its way through five miles of the South Downs. What makes the walk so attractive is that there is no public road along the full length of the valley, and much of the route is actually by the riverside.

For the best views of Arundel Castle you need to look behind you soon after you join the river. Most of what you see from this viewpoint is attractive eighteenth and nineteenth-century restoration work, although the castle dates back to 1070. It has been the family home of the Dukes of Norfolk and their ancestors for 850 years. The duke holds the title Earl Marshal of England and is responsible for organising royal coronations - a not too onerous duty during the past 60 years!

Burpham lies high above the river. In fact, to reach it you must climb Jacob's Ladder or 'the seventy steps'. Tradition has it that these were much used by smugglers in the eighteenth century to bring their French brandy up the river to hide in the cellars of the inn before later moving it on to the gentlemen's clubs of London.

The path up to St Mary's Church is named after Marjorie Hay, the daughter of Tickner Edwardes who was vicar of Burpham until1935. The story has it that Marjorie slipped and

fell on her way to church one morning and the reverend paid to have the path improved. He was a keen beekeeper and his book 'The Lore of the Honey Bee' has become a classic of its kind.

After crossing the railway for the second time there is a splendid view of South Stoke village across the river. At the end of a 2½-mile (4 kilometre) cul-de-sac, this is a delightfully remote place. The church of St Leonard is nearly a thousand years old and services are still lit by candlelight. The path from here to neighbouring North Stoke crosses a splendid new bridge built in 2009 by soldiers of the 70 Ghurkha Field Support Squadron.

THE BASICS

Distance: 5½ miles / 8.7km

Gradient: A mainly flat river walk with one flight of steps and a gentle hill

Severity: Moderate/strenuous

Approx. time to walk: 2¼ hours

Stiles: Fourteen

Maps: OS Explorer 121 (Arundel and Pulborough); OS Landranger 197 (Chichester and the South Downs)

Path description: Good riverside paths with quiet country lanes but lots of stiles

Start Point: Arundel Railway Station (GR TQ 024064)

Parking: Pay and display in station car park (PC BN18 9PH)

Dog friendly: If they can manage the stiles and are on a lead at start and finish

Public Toilets: At the train station and at the Bridge Inn

Nearest food: Riverside tearooms or the Bridge Inn or lots back in Arundel town

Look out for: Arundel Castle, Museum and Cathedral; also Amberley Museum and Heritage Centre

12 ARUN VALLEY WALK

ROUTE

1. From the station car park, walk towards the main road. Keep on the left side of the A27 until you reach the pedestrian crossing. Cross here, and follow the road into Arundel. Just after the bed and breakfast called 'Portreeves' follow a public footpath sign to the right to the river and turn right.

2. Follow the river bank as it sweeps gracefully left and northwards. After 1 kilometre (just over half a mile) the path swings away from the river to a kissing gate and the railway level crossing. Cross carefully, and immediately after the white house turn left, following a broad track into the woods. Follow to reach a kissing gate and walk ahead with an open field on your right and a line of poplar trees ahead. Cross a dropping stile beneath the trees and walk diagonally across the field to a 'rife'.

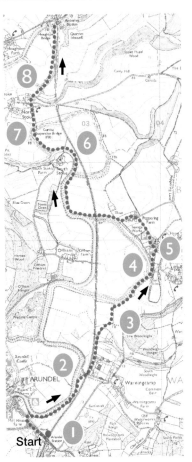

3. Turn half-right over a concrete bridge and in 30 metres look for a fingerpost to your left. Cross a stile on your left through a gap in the hedge, and follow a grassy path northwards along the right-hand side of a field to reach the bank of the river. Cross a stile onto the bank and turn right over a second stile to follow this 'elbow' of the River Arun. In 100 metres go left over two stiles, crossing a deep rife and a couple more stiles on the bank to the foot of 'Jacob's Ladder'.

4. Climb the steps ahead of you, and at the top follow the enclosed narrow path past Burpham Playing Fields. Pass to the left of the pavilion to reach the George Inn, and (if it's still too early for refreshment) continue straight ahead into the churchyard of St Mary's Church, following the Marjorie Hay path.

5. Pass to the left of the church and emerge via the kissing gate onto the tarmac road; continue ahead northwards to reach Peppering Farm. At the T-junction here

turn left, going downhill past the 'cul-de-sac' sign. This becomes a stone farm track with cottages to the right. At the bottom of the hill, turn right and cross a stile beside a metal gate to follow the raised bank along the riverside to two more high stiles over the railway line. Cross the line with care and stay on the raised bank as the river sweeps broadly right. After 750 metres cross a stile into a bushy area and exit over a second stile back onto the riverbank. There is now a lovely view of South Stoke across the river as you swing left to approach an iron bridge with a track leading out of the village.

6   Cross a stile onto the track, and ignoring the bridge, pass through a kissing gate in front of you to continue on the same side of the river as before. The path curves a little left and in 200 metres approaches a line of trees to the right. Just before reaching a metal gate on the riverbank, turn right off the bank towards these trees and pass through a kissing gate to enter the woods following a yellow footpath arrow. Walk carefully along this narrow, raised path through the trees to finally reach a splendid suspension bridge, recently rebuilt with the help of the Ghurkhas.

7   Take this footbridge over the 'old' river, and in a further 50 metres a kissing gate leads into an open field and a clear path heading gently ahead uphill. At the top of the rise, pass through two kissing gates straight ahead to walk behind a row of cottages and emerge onto a tarmac road. Turn left and in 10 metres, beside the telephone kiosk, turn immediately right heading northwards and downhill.

8   Follow this quiet lane for just over 1 kilometre to reach Houghton Bridge with the welcoming sight of the Bridge Inn and the Riverside Tearooms. Continue along the main road under the railway bridge and turn right into Amberley Station, where a normally regular and reliable train service will return you one stop down the line to Arundel Station.

13 SLINDON

THE FORGE IN SLINDON OPENED IN 2012 THROUGH COMMUNITY EFFORT AND CO-OPERATION. AS THE NAME SUGGESTS THE BUILDING ORIGINALLY HOUSED THE VILLAGE BLACKSMITH, AND THERE ARE MANY REMINDERS OF THIS. THE SHOP SELLS A WIDE RANGE OF PRODUCTS AND THE CAFÉ PROVIDES LOVELY CAKES AND MEALS. THE BUILDING ALSO ACTS AS A LOCAL INFORMATION POINT, INCLUDING AN INTERACTIVE TOUCH-SCREEN INSTALLED BY THE NATIONAL TRUST.

Many villages in Sussex claim to be the 'cradle of cricket' and there is no doubt that Slindon has a very old cricket club. The distinctive village sign commemorates this. It was put up to mark the millennium by the Slindon Pudding Club, a group of villagers who raise money to help needy members of the community and fund village initiatives. Slindon produced some great eighteenth-century cricketers; Richard Newland was a particularly fine left-handed batsman and bowler. In the 1740s an all-England team was beaten by 'poore little Slyndon ... in almost one innings'.

In the time of Queen Elizabeth I it was forbidden to worship as a Roman Catholic. At the time, the family living in Slindon House were Catholic and their successors remained so until emancipation in 1829. They would worship in secret and Slindon House had its own 'priest's hole' with a secret passage allowing the priest to escape through the cellars. The death penalty for being a Catholic priest was removed in the 1680s, but those who refused to give up Catholicism were subject to heavy fines and taxes. Many families converted to Protestantism, but Slindon was one of the few places in Sussex that included tiny congregations of Catholics.

The Catholic church of St Richard was built in the 1860s. Anne, Countess of Newburgh, who lived in Slindon House, was a devout Catholic and endowed both this church and one in Chichester – also dedicated to St Richard.

The National Trust now owns and manages the 3,500-acre Slindon Estate. It was bequeathed to them in the 1950s with the condition that 'the whole be maintained as far as possible as a Sussex estate'. They also own around two-thirds of the houses in the village, as well as Slindon House. When the National Trust surveyor visited the estate in 1944 he described the park and estate as 'a dream of beauty but ... the house is a travesty'. Although originally Elizabethan, it has been vastly altered, resulting in the flint building we see today.

The Countess of Newburgh had Nore Folly built around 1814. She asked an unemployed bricklayer, Samuel Refoy, if he could build her a copy of an arch shown in a print brought back from Italy. She was so pleased with the result that he was made estate bricklayer at Slindon House. The folly was later used by the countess for picnics and shooting parties.

The walk passes through some attractive woodland. The National Trust actively manages these woods by thinning the trees to let more light through for wildflowers and other woodland plants to grow. They also deliberately leave piles of brush and logs to provide a rich habitat for wildlife.

THE BASICS

Distance: 4½ miles / 7.2km

Gradient: Steady climb all the way to the folly; smaller hills thereafter

Severity: Moderate

Approx. time to walk: 2hrs

Stiles: None

Maps: OS Explorer 121 (Arundel and Pulborough); OS Landranger 197 (Chichester and the South Downs)

Path description: Good farm tracks and quiet country lanes

Start Point: The Forge Café and Shop, Reynolds Lane, Slindon (GR SU 966079)

Parking: Free public car park beside the café (PC BN18 0QT)

Dog friendly: Yes

Public Toilets: In the café/shop

Nearest food: The Forge Café, Slindon or the Spur Inn on the A29

Look out for: Slindon Pumpkins - a celebration of all things pumpkin, Denmans Gardens and Fontwell Park Racecourse

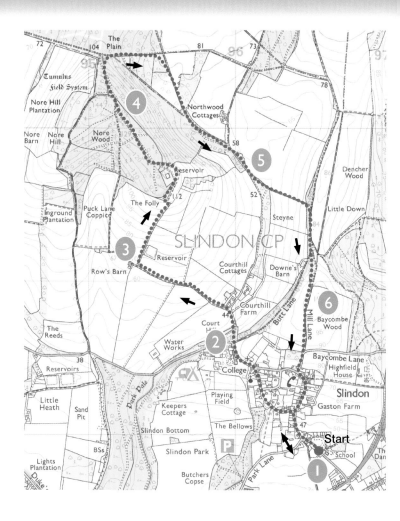

ROUTE

1. From the car park, walk past the café up towards the centre of the village, and on passing the village sign continue to your right up School Hill. In 200 metres, at the next road junction, turn left into Church Hill and walk past the village pond and St Mary's Church to a T-junction at the top of the hill.

2. Turn left past the Catholic church and just after the entrance to Slindon College, beside the speed de-restriction sign, turn right down an unmarked but clear path between the trees (not the bridleway through the gate). At the bottom continue ahead on the tarmac lane for 100 metres, then turn left on a broad farm track following the yellow footpath sign.

3. After 600 metres, before reaching a stone barn on the left, look for a fingerpost indicating a footpath going uphill to the right. Follow this grassy track almost to the top of the hill, where a sharp left turn brings you to the folly. Leave here on the farm track over the brow of the hill to pass through a metal gate onto a pleasant forest ride.

4. In 400 metres reach a T-junction and turn right on the descending bridleway. In a further 75 metres, where the path forks, keep right, heading more steeply downhill to reach a crossing bridleway at the bottom of the hill and turn right. At the edge of the wood reach a four-armed fingerpost; turn right again on the crossing bridleway. Soon reach a tarmac road and continue ahead, slightly to the right.

5. Take care here – in 250 metres, fork left into the trees, away from the road, following a blue bridleway sign. Follow through the woods then uphill across an open field, and at the T-junction at the top of the hill turn right. There follow two close forks in the bridleway: at the first keep right; at the second keep left. You should now be climbing slightly through the trees.

6. Follow the track over the rise, and as the rooftops of Slindon come into view, drop down to join the public road which is Mill Lane. Continue straight ahead to the T-junction in the village and turn left. Follow the road as it swings right down School Hill and becomes Reynolds Lane, with the welcoming sight of the Forge Café.

14 DUNCTON

DUNCTON MILL TAKES ADVANTAGE OF ONE OF THE MANY CHALK STREAMS RUNNING FROM THE FOOT OF THE DOWNS. THE MILL WAS ONCE USED FOR MILLING CORN AND CLOTH. IT IS NOW A COMMERCIAL TROUT FARM AND FISHERY RAISING BOTH BROWN AND RAINBOW TROUT. THESE ARE SOLD TO RESTOCK LARGE RESERVOIRS AND SMALL SYNDICATE WATERS, AS WELL AS STOCKING THE LARGE LAKES FOR FISHING ON SITE. THE FISHERY ALSO HAS FACILITIES FOR HOSTING WEDDINGS, CONFERENCES AND OTHER SPECIAL EVENTS.

Duncton was famous for the old custom of 'wassailing', which continued here until the 1920s. Early in January the wassailers would visit each house in the village with an orchard, and surrounding the trees they would chant a rhyme and blow their horns. Much cider was drunk on these occasions. The ceremony drove away any evil spirits lurking in the trees and ensured a good apple crop for the coming season.

The current house at Burton Park dates from 1828, following the partial destruction of an older house by fire. During the Second World War it was occupied by the army. The house and some of the grounds were then sold to St Michael's School, and it remained a boarding school for girls until it was bought in the early 1990s by three development companies. The house was converted into private apartments and new dwellings were built in the gardens. The park is privately owned and the house is a Grade I listed building.

Beside the house is the tiny church of St Richard, one of the smallest in Sussex, and still in regular use. Originally built around 1075, it has been altered and restored over the centuries. It is well worth pausing to visit, not least to admire the unusual wall painting reputed to be of St Wilgefortis, also known as St Uncumber. This unfortunate young woman was the daughter of a Portuguese nobleman who had been promised in marriage by her father to a pagan king. To prevent the wedding, Uncumber took a vow of virginity and prayed that she would be made repulsive. Her prayers were answered – she sprouted a luxurious beard, which quickly ended the engagement. Her father was so angry he had her crucified! During the fourteenth century she was venerated by those seeking relief from tribulations, especially by women who wished to be 'disencumbered' of abusive husbands.

This walk takes in small parts of two waymarked trails. The Serpent Trail runs from Haslemere to Petersfield. These towns are only 15 miles (25 km) apart by road, but the trail takes a 64-mile serpentine route across many areas of heathland. A guide can be downloaded from www.southdowns.gov.uk providing information about the plants and creatures to be found in these important habitats.

West Sussex has been home to many authors and featured in many novels, and the West Sussex Literary Trail traces a pretty 65-mile (110 kilometre) route from Horsham to Chichester; the trail guide brings to life the many literary connections along the way (www.westsussexliterarytrail.co.uk).

THE BASICS

Distance: 2¾ miles / 4.2km

Gradient: One short, easy climb from the fishery; otherwise flat

Severity: Easy

Approx. time to walk: 1½ hours

Stiles: None

Maps: OS Explorer 121 (Arundel and Pulborough); OS Landranger 197 (Chichester and the South Downs)

Path description: Hard surface drives and good footpaths

Start Point: Cricketers Inn, Duncton (GR SU 960170)

Parking: Lay-by in front of the Cricketers Inn, Duncton (PC GU28 0LB)

Dog friendly: Yes

Public Toilets: Only at the inn

Nearest food: Cricketers Inn

Look out for: Bignor Roman Villa and Petworth House (NT)

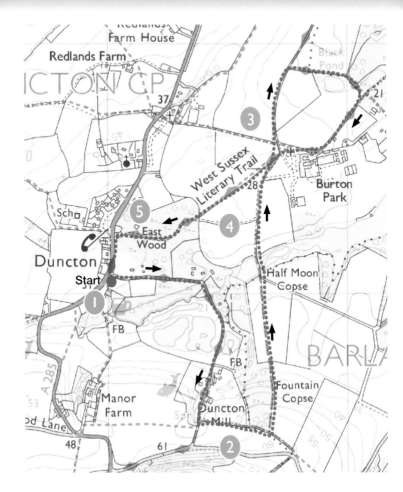

ROUTE

1. From the lay-by, walk northwards along the grass verge beside the road and take the first bridleway right. Follow this tarmac driveway over a stream and up to Duncton Fisheries. After admiring the rainbow trout in this beautiful spot, continue up the drive and in 75 metres turn left following a bridleway uphill through the trees.

2. Pass by an old orchard before the track opens out with fine views to the north, and

take the next bridleway left down the side of a large open field. This path crosses the headwaters of the first of the Burton Mill Ponds before an iron gate leads into another open field and onto the drive past Burton Park Mansion.

3. On reaching the small church of St Richard, take the bridleway left and follow this stony track northwards towards an isolated farmhouse. In 300 metres turn right, following the Serpents Trail towards a large clump of trees. Pass beside Black Pond to emerge through a kissing gate onto the tarmac drive beneath a splendid sweet chestnut tree. Here, turn right back towards the mansion.

4. On passing St Richard's Church, continue along the drive for a further 50 metres and fork right, following the yellow footpath arrow on a narrow path between two fences (the West Sussex Literary Trail). On reaching the driveway once more, turn right and follow this through the trees to the main road.

5. Turn left and walk down the grass verge on the left side of the road to the welcoming sight of the Cricketers Inn.

15 SINGLETON

THE CHURCH IN SINGLETON IS MENTIONED IN THE
DOMESDAY BOOK OF 1086. THE TOWER IS SAXON AND IS BUILT
OF PARTIALLY RENDERED RUBBLE; THE BATTLEMENTS WERE
PROBABLY ADDED LATER. THE CHURCH WAS ORIGINALLY
DEDICATED TO ST MARY, BUT DUE TO AN ERROR IN THE
NINETEENTH CENTURY IT WAS ATTRIBUTED TO ST JOHN THE
EVANGELIST UNTIL 1979, WHEN IT ONCE AGAIN BECAME ST
MARY'S.

The walk follows a wide valley formed by the River Lavant – a Celtic river-name meaning 'gliding one'. This rises in a pond in the village of East Dean to the east and flows through Chichester to the harbour. It is a winterbourne, meaning that traditionally it flows mostly in winter when there is plenty of rain. Over a few very dry years the Lavant virtually disappeared, but in recent wet years it has caused major floods in Singleton and Chichester, leading one newspaper to call it 'the little river that roared'.

St Roche's Hill, better known as the Trundle, was occupied in Palaeolithic times. It was later a Neolithic 'causewayed camp' and then an Iron Age hill fort, the name the Trundle coming from an Old English word for circle. St Roche is the patron saint of healing. Born in 1295, he worked with plague sufferers and there was once a chapel dedicated to him on top of

the hill, although it was a ruin by 1570. His saint's day is on 16 August, and every year a service takes place on the chapel site.

Levin Down nature reserve is managed by the Sussex Wildlife Trust and is a Site of Special Scientific Interest (SSSI). The reason that Levin is such an important site for wildlife is suggested in its name, which is derived from 'leave-alone hill' – the land has never been intensively farmed. The down is the largest area of chalk heath in Sussex and is a rare and important habitat. It is still a managed landscape, with scrub clearance and grazing to maintain the right balance of plants. An information sheet can be found at www.sussexwildlifetrust.org.uk.

The impressive finger post at Hunters Gate commemorates the most famous day in the history of the Charlton Hunt – the 'Grand Chase'. The hounds ran continuously from eight in the morning until six at night. The Duke of Richmond was so pleased to have ridden the whole day that he sent his servants out with a cartwheel to check the distance – 57 miles. The current

post replaced an older one from the 1970s when a hunt was still going strong in this area, providing directions for riders who had lost their way.

The New Lipchis Way is a 39-mile (62-kilometre) trail from Liphook on the Hampshire/ West Sussex border to East Head at the entrance to Chichester Harbour; a leaflet is available from: www.newlipchisway.co.uk.

The distinctive white building of Goodwood racecourse dates from 1979, although further stands have been added since. Horse racing has taken place here since 1801 when the third Duke of Richmond introduced racing for the officers of the Sussex Militia, of which he was Colonel. Nineteen events a year are now held here including the sparkling 'Glorious Goodwood' – a sporting highlight in the social calendar.

THE BASICS

Distance: 3¼ miles / 5.2km

Gradient: Two easy ascents and one slightly steeper descent

Severity: Moderate

Approx. time to walk: 1½ hours

Stiles: One

Maps: OS Explorer 120 (Chichester); OS Landranger 197 (Chichester and the South Downs)

Path description: Mostly grassy tracks; one section of narrow path on Levin Down

Start Point: The Partridge Inn, Singleton (GR SU 877131)

Parking: Roadside parking near the Partridge Inn (PC PO18 0EY)

Dog friendly: If they can manage stiles and should be on leads because of cattle and sheep throughout the walk

Public Toilets: Only at the inn

Nearest food: Teashop or Partridge Inn in Singleton

Look out for: Goodwood Racecourse and the Weald and Downland Open Air Museum

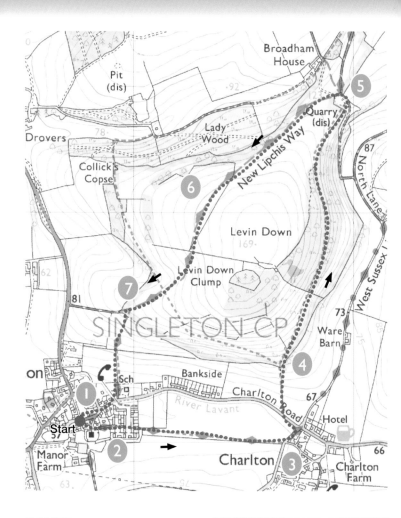

ROUTE

1. With your back to the pub entrance turn left to walk along the road heading eastwards for 50 metres. At Easter Cottage turn right towards the church.

2. In front of the church, turn left to walk past the children's play area and through The Leys to follow a yellow footpath arrow into a large open field. Walk straight ahead for 15 minutes to reach a public road.

3. Turn left, and at the road junction turn left again for 75 metres to reach a kissing gate on the right. Go through this and follow the footpath uphill to a gate, where there is a bench with fine views of the Lavant Valley and the two aerials atop the Trundle opposite.

4. Pass immediately through a second gate and turn half-right past the information board. A further gate leads to a fork in the path; keep left, going more steeply uphill. This well-trodden path leads around the open hillside of Levin Down and eventually enters a wooded area where a stile and a gate lead out onto open downland. Here, turn right, heading downhill to the lower right-hand corner of the field.

5. Pass briefly through a small wood to emerge onto a wide crossing bridleway and turn left uphill to reach Hunters Gate with its splendid fingerpost. Follow the arm pointing towards Singleton, through a metal gate and along a bridleway. The route is towards the far corner of the tree line on your right, over the western flank of Levin Down.

6. As you reach the highest point of the walk, join a wire fence on your right and descend gently through a gate with fine views of Goodwood racecourse in the distance. The bridleway curves slowly right around the hillside and goes straight over a crossing footpath, following the New Lipchis Way towards a clump of trees.

7. On reaching the first tree on your right, take the left fork in the track leading down to a kissing gate and then almost immediately go through a second gate with views of the village directly below. Follow the clear path quite steeply downhill to pass beside the primary school and exit onto the public road. Turn right, and at the fork in the road, the tearooms are to your right and the inn to your left.

THE MAJORITY OF THIS WALK IS WITHIN THE WEST DEAN ESTATE, WHICH IS OWNED AND MANAGED BY THE EDWARD JAMES FOUNDATION, A CHARITABLE EDUCATIONAL TRUST. WEST DEAN IS RECORDED IN THE DOMESDAY BOOK AS A HUNTING PARK. IT WAS HELD FOR SEVERAL CENTURIES BY THE EARLS OF ARUNDEL AND THE DUKES OF NORFOLK, CHANGING HANDS A NUMBER OF TIMES UNTIL WILLIAM JAMES BOUGHT THE ESTATE IN 1891. AT THE TURN OF THE TWENTIETH CENTURY THE ESTATE WAS WELL KNOWN FOR ITS LARGE SHOOTING PARTIES, ATTENDED BY KING EDWARD VII AND MANY OTHER ROYAL VISITORS. ON WILLIAM'S DEATH IN 1912 THE ESTATE WAS INHERITED BY HIS ONLY SON, EDWARD.

The estate is mainly farmed, providing a range of arable crops and grazed by cattle and sheep. However, one third is woodland and it is mostly through this that our walk takes place. Pheasant and partridge shoots are still an important part of the local economy and many young birds can be seen after their release in the summer.

Part of the walk is through ancient woodland, meaning that the area has been continuously wooded since 1600 or before. It was around this date that fairly accurate estate maps began to be produced, showing areas of existing woodland, and widespread tree-planting began. Woods known to exist by that date were almost certainly natural in composition. However, this does not mean that such woodland has been undisturbed or unmanaged; the woods here have been used for the production of hurdles for fencing and firewood and charcoal by coppicing.

Forestry remains an important commercial activity on the West Dean estate and piles of logs can be seen as the walk progresses. The severe storm of 1987 and another in 1990 devastated the woodland, blowing over historic 150-year-old beech trees as well as trees almost ready for commercial felling. Massive clearance and replanting was necessary, and the estate is once again a successful woodland enterprise. As well as selling wood commercially, it fuels a biomass heating system that supplies all the heating and hot water needs of West Dean College (another part of the estate).

The Royal Oak at Hooksway is a delightful old building with a pretty garden. Dating from the 1400s, it has long been a pub or alehouse. The grandson of one licensee described the life of his grandparents here at the end of the nineteenth century. William Woods was a gamekeeper but was attacked one day by poachers, which ended his career. Instead he became the licensee at the Royal Oak. He spent his time looking after the woodland and pastures, growing food and rearing animals to feed his family while his wife Martha ran the pub. She managed to stay 'open all hours', ignoring the licensing laws, by keeping the local police constable well supplied with free beer and produce from the farm. Look out for the resident ghost of William Shepherd, who was a sheep rustler on the South Downs around 1680. A group of angry farmers chased him across the downs and he was eventually shot after taking refuge here in the pub.

THE BASICS

Distance: 2¼ miles / 3.2km

Gradient: Short, steepish section of the South Downs Way

Severity: Short walk but with a moderate climb

Approx. time to walk: 1¼ hours

Stiles: None

Maps: OS Explorer 120 (Chichester); OS Landranger 197 (Chichester and the South Downs)

Path description: A broad 'bostal' (downland path) and good woodland paths

Start Point: The Royal Oak, Hooksway (GR SU 815162)

Parking: Car park of the Royal Oak, by kind permission (PC PO18 9JZ)

Dog friendly: Yes

Public Toilets: Only at the inn

Nearest food: The Royal Oak – please do pop in to say thanks for the parking!

Look out for: Uppark House and Garden (NT)

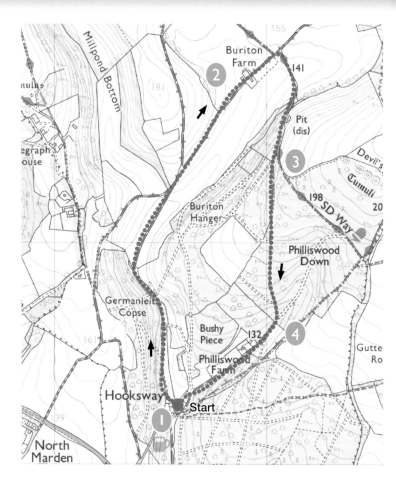

ROUTE

1. Take the bridleway leading from the back of the car park, following the blue arrow northwards along the valley floor. After 700 metres, pass through a gate into more open countryside. At a second gate the path begins to rise and becomes a 'restricted byway'.

2. Continue straight ahead along this classic chalk bostal, past Buriton Farm to join the South Downs Way (SDW) coming in from your left. Just a few metres further on turn sharp right, following the national trail. The bridleway climbs steadily into the trees, and 250 metres after entering the trees you must look carefully to your right for a fingerpost indicating a bridleway glancing away to the right.

3. Turn right here off the SDW and continue to climb more gently before levelling off and starting a gentle descent through the trees. The path broadens and steepens then makes a half-right as it passes several log piles in the woods.

4. Continue past Philliswood Barn, and just after Philliswood Cottage return to the Royal Oak car park.

DROXFORD'S HISTORY STRETCHES BACK WELL OVER A THOUSAND YEARS WHEN RECORDS SHOW THAT DROCENESFORDA WAS GRANTED TO WINCHESTER'S ST SWITHUN'S PRIORY BY KING EGBERT OF WESSEX IN 826. MUCH MORE RECENTLY THE VILLAGE PLAYED HOST TO SEVERAL INFLUENTIAL FIGURES DURING THE SECOND WORLD WAR. IN THE DAYS BEFORE THE D-DAY INVASION, SIR WINSTON CHURCHILL AND THE ALLIED CHIEFS INCLUDING EISENHOWER AND DE GAULLE HELD MEETINGS IN A TRAIN CARRIAGE AT DROXFORD STATION; THE MEETINGS ARE COMMEMORATED BY A SMALL PLAQUE ON THE SEAT NEAR THE START OF THE WALK.

The Meon Valley Railway, which opened in 1903, ran between Alton and Fareham. Unfortunately, passenger services were withdrawn in 1955 and the line closed in 1968. The Church of St Mary and All Saints dates from the mid-twelfth century; step inside to see the colourful stained glass windows including a recent one celebrating the new Millennium.

From Droxford, the walk heads south before crossing the picturesque River Meon to visit the peaceful village of Soberton whose name was used in the peerage of Baron Anson of Soberton, bestowed on the eighteenth-century Admiral of the Fleet George Anson. Call at the twelfth-century Church of St Peter to see a stone coffin in the churchyard which is believed to date from Roman times, while inside the church is a plaque and ship's bell from HMS Soberton, a minesweeper and fishery protection vessel launched in 1956.

Just to the north of the church is Soberton Towers. Built in the late nineteenth century by Colonel Charles Brome Bashford, the house has also served as a school and living quarters for Wrens from HMS Mercury based near East Meon. The last part of the walk heads north along the east side of the valley before crossing over the river again to arrive back at Droxford.

THE BASICS

Distance: 4½ miles / 7km

Gradient: A couple of easy ascents and descents

Severity: Easy, though river can flood in winter

Approx. time to walk: 2¼ hours

Stiles: Ten

Map: OS Explorer OL3 (Meon Valley)

Path description: Paths and tracks, country lanes, some road crossings

Start Point: The A32 in Droxford opposite Park Lane (GR SU 606182)

Parking: Parking area on A32 opposite Park Lane in Droxford (PC SO32 3PA)

Dog friendly: If they can manage the stiles and should be on leads

Toilets: none on walk

Nearest food: Bakers Arms and White Horse Inn at Droxford; White Lion at Soberton

Look out for: Bishop's Waltham Palace (EH), Beacon Hill and Old Winchester Hill

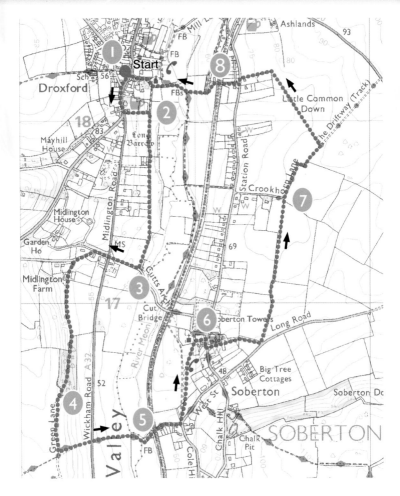

ROUTE

1   From the parking area cross over the A32 and turn left, following the road through the village past the White Horse Inn. Where the pavement ends, cross the road and continue for a short way before turning left at the driveway opposite Swanmore Road. Follow the enclosed path downhill.

2   Turn right over the stile and follow the left-hand field edge. Cross two stiles in the corner and keep ahead, now following the fence on the right. Later head across the field and over a stile beside a gate in the far left corner. Continue along the left-hand field margin and leave through a kissing gate.

3   Turn right up the lane to a crossroads with the A32. With care, cross over and follow the lane opposite for 200 metres to a slight right-hand bend at the entrance to Midlington Farm; go left along the bridleway. Follow the track for 800 metres, later heading uphill to enter a field beside a seat.

4   After admiring the view, continue along the hedge on the right, and shortly after the power line turn left down across the field. Go through hedge gaps either side of the A32 (cross with care) and continue through the field. Go through a kissing gate and keep ahead to cross the footbridge over the River Meon.

5   Follow the riverside path for a short way, go under the old railway bridge and follow the lane uphill with houses on the right. At the T-junction, turn left through a gate to enter a field. Follow the path northwards through three fields separated by a kissing gate and stile, aiming for the church. Cross a stile in the top right corner – to the left is the church – and turn right along the lane to the main street in Soberton beside the seventeenth-century White Lion pub.

6   Turn right for 50 metres and just before the house on the left (Great Down), turn left along the narrow path. Keep ahead past a barn, follow the track and go through a large gate with a lane beyond. Immediately turn left over a stile and follow the left-hand field margin. Cross a stile and follow the fence on the left; later keep ahead across the field.

7   Cross a stile and follow the hedge-lined track (Crookhorn Lane) straight on as it turns right and left. Keep ahead for 100 metres before turning left; follow the grassy strip between fields and then bear left alongside the trees on the left. Cross the stile at the corner and turn left along the lane for 25 metres before turning right along the track (bridleway).

8   Cross the old railway bridge and follow the track, go through a gate and keep ahead across the field for 25m. Go through two small gates at the trees and continue downhill with the field edge on the left. Cross two footbridges over the River Meon and continue towards the church. Keep ahead beside the brick wall and turn right through a kissing gate, following the path past the church as it swings left back to the start; 175 metres to the right along the A32 is the Bakers Arms.

18 WEST MEON

THE VILLAGE OF WEST MEON, TUCKED IN THE PICTURESQUE
MEON VALLEY THROUGH WHICH THE RIVER MEON FLOWS
ON ITS JOURNEY SOUTH TO THE SOLENT, HAS LINKS WITH
LORD'S CRICKET GROUND AND A NOTORIOUS SPY. THIS IS AN
AREA WITH A HISTORY STRETCHING BACK MILLENNIA, FROM
THE IRON AGE HILL FORT ON OLD WINCHESTER HILL TO THE
REMAINS OF A ROMAN VILLA HIDDEN IN LIPPEN WOOD.

Back in the present, the walk sets out from the village, meandering through fields and woods before following the Meon Valley. Soon a lovely view of West Meon opens out, dominated by the church tower and surrounded by a patchwork landscape.

Call in at the Gothic Revival-styled Church of St John the Evangelist, built in the 1840s by the noted architect Sir George Gilbert Scott, to see some colourful stained glass windows.

In the churchyard is the grave of Thomas Lord (1755–1832), the founder of Lord's Cricket Ground in London; Thomas, who was originally from Yorkshire, spent his retirement in West Meon. The parents of *Rural Rides* author William Cobbett also lie in churchyard. A less celebrated incumbent is Guy Burgess (1911–1963), a member of the 'Cambridge Five' who operated as Soviet spies from the 1930s to the 1950s; his ashes were interred at night to avoid press coverage.

From the church the route meanders through the village following Station Road – a reminder of a bygone era. The Meon Valley Railway, which opened in 1903, followed the valley on its journey from Alton to Fareham. Sadly the line closed in 1955, however, the old track bed now forms a bridle route from West Meon to Wickham.

The final leg of the walk follows the High Street, passing the Thomas Lord pub and the village shop/café before heading back to the start. Originally called the New Inn, the pub was renamed in 1955 in Thomas' honour.

THE BASICS

Distance: 5¼ miles / 8.4km

Gradient: Some easy ups and downs

Severity: Easy, can get muddy around Brockwood Copse

Approx. time to walk: 2½ hours

Stiles: Three

Map: OS Explorer OL32 (Winchester, New Alresford and East Meon)

Path description: Country lanes, some road crossings, paths and tracks

Start Point: Village hall and recreation ground in West Meon (GR SU 641242)

Parking: Village Hall along Headon View in West Meon, just off the A32 (PC GU32 1LH)

Dog friendly: If they can manage stiles and should be on leads in fields

Toilets: None on the walk

Nearest food: The Thomas Lord and village shop/café, both in West Meon

Look out for: Hinton Ampner (NT), Beacon Hill and Old Winchester Hill

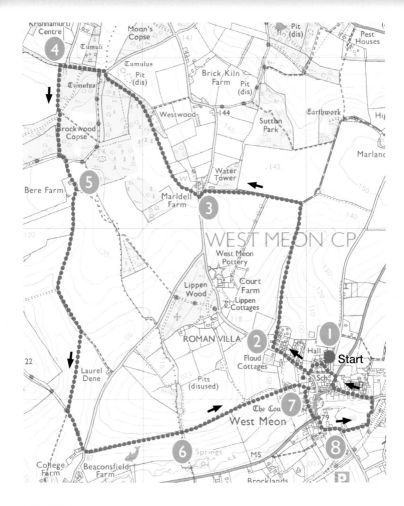

ROUTE

1   From the village hall, head down the entrance drive and follow the road as it swings right. At the end of the road, keep ahead along the narrow path and turn left down to a lane opposite the church. Turn right along the lane passing Floud Lane (left), and just after Long Priors (right) turn right along a track (signposted for Hill View).

2   Keep ahead into the field and follow the left-hand margin uphill. At the top go through a gap in the hedge and turn left along the hedge-lined track (bridleway) to a lane at Marldell Farm.

3   Turn left for 25 metres to Marldell Farm, then turn right along the enclosed bridleway. Keep ahead into the woods to a junction and continue straight on along the bridleway, passing a wooden electricity pole; this area is a great for bluebells in the spring. Turn left along the road for 250 metres, and just after the junction turn left past a large gate.

4   Follow the left-hand field edge and then continue southwards through the trees to a defined track. Turn left then right and go through a gate, following the track just to the left of the house at Bere Farm. After the buildings, keep ahead long the driveway (track) for half a mile to a footpath sign.

5   Turn right here and follow the path down across the large field to the opposite side. Turn left along the track to a road and keep ahead for 10 metres before turning left up some steps. Cross the stile and follow the left-hand fence to the top-left field corner.

6   Cross the stile and keep ahead; West Meon soon comes into view. Head downhill, exit the field and keep ahead along the road (Floud Lane) for 20 metres, and then take the narrow path between high fences. Cross the stone stile and keep ahead through the churchyard to a cross-path junction beside the grave of Thomas Lord; to the left is the Church of St John the Evangelist.

7   Turn right down the path, leave the churchyard and continue down the enclosed path, soon crossing a driveway and then the River Meon to reach the main road (A32). Cross with care and turn left then right along Station Road. Keep to the lane as it swings left then right, and just before the entrance to the Meon Valley Trail car park (the site of the former railway station), turn left at the footpath sign.

8   Follow the narrow path between walls, then alongside the fence (left) as it swings left down to a footbridge. Cross this and keep ahead to cross another footbridge. Turn left along the High Street, soon passing the Thomas Lord pub and the shop/café to reach a junction with the A32 beside a thatched cottage. Turn right for 50 metres, then turn left, crossing the road with care to take the lane opposite. After 40 metres, turn left along Headon Way and keep right then right again, back to the village hall.

THE WALK STARTS IN THE LITTLE HAMLET OF EXTON, PASSING THE TWELFTH-CENTURY CHURCH OF ST PETER AND ST PAUL. INSIDE, ON THE EAST WALL BEHIND THE ALTAR IS A STENCILLED WALL PAINTING AND THREE STAINED GLASS WINDOWS DESIGNED BY CHARLES SPOONER IN THE MID-1890S.

Next up is Corhampton, home to a lovely little church dating back to the late Saxon period; the church is unusual in that it has no dedication. The final village stop-off is Meonstoke, home to the Bucks Head pub and St Andrew's Church, which dates from 1230 and is built in an Early English style.

Soon the walk crosses over the former Meon Valley railway which connected Alton and Fareham. The line opened in 1903 and closed to passenger traffic in 1955; now the old track bed from West Meon to Wickham forms the 10-mile Meon Valley Trail – great for a walk or cycle ride. The shorter walk follows part of the former route.

From here the full-length walk starts a gradual climb to reach the heights of Old Winchester Hill (197 metres); despite its name, the hill is actually some 11 miles from Winchester. The hill, part of a designated National Nature Reserve, consists of a large area of unimproved chalk grassland that is home to a varied flora and fauna including several types of orchid and a range of butterflies including the chalkhill blue.

Crowning the summit are the remains of an Iron Age hill fort built around 2500 years ago, as well as some earlier Bronze Age barrows or burial mounds (4500 to 3500 BC). From this lofty location there is a great panoramic view to the north-west across the valley to Beacon Hill and south down to the sea. The final leg of the walk follows the South Downs Way back to the start.

THE BASICS

Distance: 5½ miles / 8.8km (shorter option: 3 miles / 4.7km)

Gradient: One ascent and descent up Old Winchester Hill

Severity: Moderate due to Old Winchester Hill

Approx. time to walk: 2¾ hours (shorter walk: 1¼ hours)

Stiles: Seven

Map: OS Explorer OL3 (Meon Valley)

Path description: Paths and tracks, country lanes and road crossings

Start Point: Small parking area at junction of Church Lane and A32 in Exton (GR SU 617212)

Parking: Lay-by at junction of Church Lane and A32 in Exton (PC SO32 3NU), about 2½ miles south of West Meon

Dog friendly: If they can manage the stiles and should be on leads

Toilets: None on the walk

Nearest food: The Shoe at Exton; the Bucks Head at Meonstoke

Look out for: Hinton Ampner (NT) and Beacon Hill

19 MEONSTOKE WALK

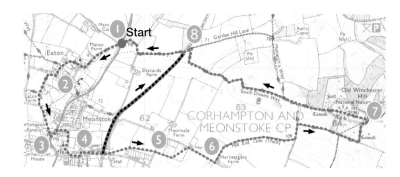

ROUTE

1   Head south-west along Church Lane towards Exton and keep right at the junction; anyone wanting an early pub stop could go left along Shoe Lane for 150 metres to reach the Shoe before returning to the junction and turning left. Continue past the Church of St Peter and St Paul, following the lane as it bends left.

2   Go right at the T-junction and then left at the next junction following Allens Farm Lane. Where this turns to the right, keep straight on along a path between the wall and fence. Pass through a kissing gate and continue along the enclosed path. Go through a gate on the left and head diagonally right across the field (roughly keeping to the same direction). Go over the stile beside the gate and continue between the buildings, one with some impressive herring-bone brick work, to join the A32 next to Corhampton Church.

3   Turn left for 75 metres, crossing the River Meon, and then right. Cross the A32 beside the village shop with care, and follow Allens Lane for 100 metres. Just after the last house on the right, turn right along a path and follow it through the churchyard; St Andrew's Church is on the right. Go through the gate and turn left along the lane to a junction beside the Buck's Head pub. Turn left up the hill to a junction.

4   Turn left, then right at the next junction following Pound Lane, soon crossing a bridge over the disused Meon Valley Railway to reach a crossroads. (For the shorter walk, from the crossroads turn left along Shavard Lane to a junction, fork left for 20 metres, and just before the old bridge turn right along the South Downs Way, following the former trackbed to Point 8.) Keep ahead over the stile beside the large gate and follow the path diagonally left across the field; ahead in the distance is Old Winchester Hill. Cross another stile and follow the field edge on the right.

5   At the corner, go left for a few metres and then right to cross stiles on either side of a lane. Continue along the field edge on the right, cross two more stiles either end of an enclosed path and then head diagonally left (north-east) across the field towards the house (on the map the right of way goes east and then north). Go through the gap in the hedge and turn right along the lane for 300 metres to Harvestgate Farm.

6   Turn left along the track (Mill End Lane) for 950m and at the hedge go left up to a bridleway junction. Go right (joining the South Downs Way) for 700 metres, ignoring a bridleway to the right and a path off to the left. At the South Downs Way sign turn left up the enclosed bridleway, following it as it bears right and left. Go through a gate and immediately turn left through another gate to reach a seat and information board on Old Winchester Hill. Bear left and soon turn right to follow a path through the middle of the earthworks to reach a trig point.

7   After admiring the view continue north-westwards and start heading downhill, going through a kissing gate and continuing down through the trees. Follow the enclosed path as it meanders its way gently downhill for about a mile, keeping straight on at the junction. At the trees, cross the footbridge and keep left to continue between the wooden fences.

8   Go up some steps to cross the disused railway next to a bridge and down steps on the other side. Keep ahead along the tree-shaded path, and at the junction with a farm track go right following the hedge-lined path. Cross a footbridge over the River Meon and then carefully cross the A32 back to the parking area.

Take a walk through history, with gardens, a High Street, a river and a magnificent cathedral. Winchester has been an important political and religious centre at various times in its history. The Romans had a large settlement here, but when they left the town declined until Alfred the Great made it his capital in the ninth century. His statue stands in the High Street, which takes the line of the old Roman Road.

Just beside the nineteenth-century bridge over the River Itchen, the eighteenth-century city mill has been restored to working order. After the Abbey Gardens you reach the elaborate Victorian Gothic Guildhall, which replaced the more modest building near the Buttercross, distinguished by the large hanging clock and a statue of Queen Anne. The fifteenth-century Buttercross, refurbished in the nineteenth century, was the spot where medieval country traders sold their goods.

At the end of the High Street the fortified twelfth-century Westgate is now a museum. Just around the corner is the thirteenth-century Great Hall, which is all that remains of the castle. Go in to have a look at the round table. This is not the round table of Arthurian legend but a newer version, made in the thirteenth century and painted in Tudor times with King Arthur represented by a young Henry VIII.

Winchester is a walk through time but the undoubted star is Winchester Cathedral. The massive edifice of the Norman cathedral, consecrated in 1093, was a statement of power and majesty to a conquered people. It was completely re-modelled in the fourteenth

century by William of Wykeham in the Perpendicular Gothic style. However, the solid Norman pillars are still there beneath the soaring columns, and the heavy round arches are visible in the North Transept. William of Wykeham is also still there; look for his effigy in the Chantry Chapel in the nave.

Many kings and bishops were buried in the cathedral, including St Swithun, whose tomb drew thousands of pilgrims over the years. However, the most visited grave today is that of Jane Austen, the novelist, who was buried here in 1817. The stone covering her grave makes no mention of her writing, but by the 1850s it was attracting so many literary pilgrims that the verger of the cathedral was heard to ask if 'there was anything particular about that lady; so many people want to know where she is buried'.

THE BASICS

Distance: 3¼ miles / 5.2km

Gradient: Flat

Severity: Easy

Approx. time to walk: 2 hours

Stiles: None

Map: OS Explorer 132 (Winchester)

Path description: Pavements, pedestrianised streets and paths

Start Point: Chesil Street north car park (GR SU 487291)

Parking: Chesil Street north car park (PC SO23 0HU) (charges apply; free on Sundays)

Dog friendly: Yes, but keep on a lead where appropriate

Toilets: Abbey Gardens

Nearest food: River Cottage Canteen, Abbey Gardens

Look out for: Cathedral, Westgate Museum, military museums, the Great Hall and the City Mill (NT)

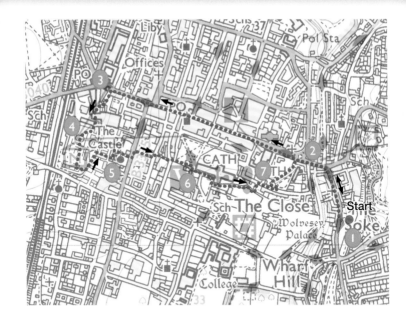

ROUTE

1. From the Chesil Street car park, exit onto Chesil Street and walk along it to reach a T-junction with Bridge Street. Turn left, cross the bridge, then continue along the High Street.

2. Keep ahead on the pedestrianised High Street, passing Middle Brook Street on the right then Market Street on the left. Take the time to stop and enjoy the many old buildings and the Buttercross, which you will find on the left by the Pentice. Then keep ahead to the Lloyds Bank building with its spectacular clock on the left. Then have a look at God Begot House opposite, and also check out the building on the left on the corner of High Street and St Thomas Street. It's now a retail outlet, but if you look closely you will see that it was once Ye Dolphin Inn. Continue to cross Southgate Street, passing Trafalgar Street on the left and the offices of BBC Radio Solent to reach the historic Westgate.

3. Just before you reach the gate bear left, heading towards the Great Hall (admission is free but donations are welcome). Walk round the Hall, look at the table then exit through a side door into the re-creation of Queen Eleanor's thirteenth-century garden. Turn right then climb up some steps, exiting onto the street and turning left to follow the signs to the cathedral.

4. Walk through the gardens of Peninsula Square surrounded by the magnificent military museum buildings, then cross to the left-hand corner to go down some steps. Turn left to pass through Beaumont Green then turn right, followed by left and right turns to pass by a church and reach a T-junction at the foot of Archery Lane.

5. Turn left, cross the road then turn right down some steps and along St Thomas' Passage, heading in the direction of the cathedral tower. At the T-junction turn left opposite Mulberry House, pass Mason's Yard on your left then turn right into Minster Lane. At the end cross over Little Minster Street then head along Great Minster Street and on into the cathedral grounds.

6. Turn right in front of the cathedral then left to walk round the outside anti-clockwise. When the path reaches the end of the cathedral, continue along to reach a T-junction and turn right along Colebrook Street.

7. A short distance along this street is River Cottage Canteen on the left. Turn left just beyond it to enter Abbey Gardens, turn left in front of River Cottage, cross a footbridge and follow either of the paths to reach a gate onto High Street. Turn right here and re-trace your outward journey to return to the car park.

iStock

MORE WALKING BOOKS FROM BRADWELL BOOKS FOR YOU TO ENJOY

BRADWELL'S POCKET WALKING GUIDES
10 Walks up to 6 miles,
suitable for all the family

Somerset
Essex
The Peak District
The Yorkshire Dales

WALKS FOR ALL AGES
20 Walks up to 6 miles,
suitable for all the family

The Black Country
Cambridgeshire
Carmarthenshire
The Chilterns
Cheshire
Co Durham
Cornwall
On Dartmoor
Devon
Dorset
Essex
Exmoor
Greater Manchester
Hampshire
Herefordshire
Kent
The Lake District
Lancashire
Leicestershire and Rutland
Lincolnshire
London Greater
Norfolk
North East Wales
Northamptonshire
Northumberland
Nottinghamshire
The Peak District
The Scottish Borders
Snowdonia & North West Wales
Somerset
Staffordshire

East Sussex
West Sussex
Vale of Glamorgan & Bridgend South
Wales
West Yorkshire
Wiltshire
The Yorkshire Dales

WALKS FOR ALL SEASONS
20 Walks up to 6 miles, suitable for all the
family throughout the year

Lincolnshire
Nottinghamshire

BRADWELLS LONGER WALKS
20 More challenging walks of up to 12 miles,
suitable for the more experienced walker

On Dartmoor
The Peak District
The Yorkshire Dales

COMING OUT IN 2017

WALKS FOR ALL AGES
20 Walks up to 6 miles,
suitable for all the family

Pembrokeshire
Suffolk
North York Moors

BRADWELL WALKING GUIDES
8 Family walks
Buxton
The Monsal Trail

Available from your
local bookshop or
order online

bradwellbooks.co.uk